HIP TO BE SQUARE

Published in 2022 by Hardie Grant Books,
an imprint of Hardie Grant Publishing

Hardie Grant Books (London)
5th & 6th Floors
52–54 Southwark Street
London SE1 1UN

Hardie Grant Books (Melbourne)
Building 1, 658 Church Street
Richmond, Victoria 3121

hardiegrantbooks.com

British Library Cataloguing-in-
Publication Data. A catalogue record
for this book is available from the
British Library.

Hip To Be Square by Katie Jones

ISBN: 978-1-78488-545-8

Publishing Director: Kajal Mistry
Senior Editor: Chelsea Edwards
Design: Claire Warner Studio
Senior Production Controller: Nikolaus Ginelli
Photography: Rachel Manns
Illustrator: Esther Coombs
Copy Editor: Lindsay Kaubi
Proofreader: Marie Clayton
Photographic assistant: Nell Gransden

Colour Reproduction by p2d
Printed and bound in China
by Leo Paper Products Ltd

20 CONTEMPORARY CROCHET DESIGNS USING 5 SIMPLE SQUARES

HIP TO BE SQUARE

KATIE JONES

Hardie Grant

BOOKS

CONTENTS

INTRODUCTION TO THE GRANNY SQUARE

Welcome to the wonderful world of the Granny Square!

The Granny Square first popped up in print in 1891 as an engraving in *The Art of Crocheting* and it has been filling homes in the form of blankets ever since. It's said that this humble motif got its name because of its clear, defined stitch pattern – which can be felt – meaning it could be produced with poor eyesight and was therefore popular with grannies. Who knows whether this is true or just an urban legend? What I do know is that wherever the name came from, the Granny Square has been a firm favourite in the crochet world ever since!

Its popularity boomed in the 1960s and 70s in the form of garments. Can we thank Paul McCartney's famous waistcoat for this? I think so! Since then, the Granny Square has come back into fashion in full force and has graced the runway for the likes of Christopher Kane, Moschino and Mui Mui, to name but a few. Its popularity has also trickled down into the must-have high-street trends. From homeware to hats, tops, jackets and dresses, this knitwear style is now no longer just reserved for winter but is a hit all year round.

With its popularity comes its pitfalls. Crochet must be produced by hand – there is no such thing as machine-made crochet. The labour-intensive nature of producing crochet means that it's a trend where the ethics of the production process get called into question. By learning to crochet, the conscientious consumer can produce their own makes, cutting out the middleman, becoming their own production process and gaining a true understanding of its value!

A traditional Granny Square is made up of clusters of three treble stitches worked in a square formation; however, the term 'granny square' is now often used more broadly to encompass most square crochet motifs.

I love a Granny Square, and I'm sure I caught the bug from my own granny, who had a multicoloured crochet blanket for every surface. Memories of summer picnics on her simple square blankets and winter nights snuggled up underneath them fill my heart with so much love! I have always been drawn to Granny Squares, first through nostalgia and then for their versatility. The combinations they can be used in and the variety of projects that can be produced from this basic motif is endless!

During my time as a crochet designer I have tried to cover as much as I can in colourful squares – ever since my mum showed me how! From filling a Selfridges window with squares and covering the chairs at my wedding to exhibiting my Granny Square designs at a V&A exhibition – I LOVE making squares. But my real passion is sharing my love of crochet and getting those squares onto your hooks!

Dive into this book and explore all things Granny Square. Hopefully you will soon be as hooked as me and agree that it's definitely *Hip to be Square*.

HAPPY HOOKIN'!

KATIE x♡x

ABOUT THIS BOOK

Come and get your square on! Don't worry if you are new to crochet, this book can take you from crochet zero to crochet hero, with projects for all skill levels!

The step-by-step instructions take you through five different square designs and clear step-by-step photos are there to guide you through making each square and using the joining methods. In addition, there are 20 projects for you and your home. The patterns are broken down into bite-sized chunks with helpful illustrations to show the construction process for each project.

The sample projects shown in the book are just the start though; the squares are designed to be interchangeable, and each project comes with tips and ideas for variations – the combinations are truly limitless!

This book is intended to work like a design handbook, supplying you with the knowledge and inspiration to grab those hooks and go wild, teaching you how to create items that can be fully customised by you, so that they are loved and last a lifetime.

If you are new to crochet, start off with a project that uses a smaller number of squares to get the hang of it – one of the accessories maybe, or the Simple Square Sweater (page 81) is a great first garment to start with. So, jump in and see what takes your fancy, grab those hooks and a notebook, and start planning your makes!

GETTING STARTED

GLOSSARY OF CROCHET TERMS

When listening to someone talk about crochet, or reading a pattern, it can seem like a whole other language, and that's because it really does have its own language of terms. In this section, we will break down those terms and their meanings and remove the mystery!

UK vs US Terminology

Understanding crochet patterns can be tricky at first because different terms mean different things in the UK and US. Most of the same stitch names are used in both the UK and US; however, the actual stitch you're working is different. This book is written in UK terminology, but here is a conversion chart showing the US counterparts.

Crochet charts and their symbols, however, are universal, so they are a helpful reference and if you are a more visual learner you may find them easier to follow. Each crochet stitch has a symbol, and these are arranged into a diagram that represents the crochet pattern. Each of the square motif patterns in this book has its own schematic, or stitch diagram, which you can also follow along with the pattern. Stitch abbreviations – which are commonly used in crochet patterns – are used for reference; however, all the patterns in this book are written in longhand to make the steps as easy to follow as possible.

Stitches and Terms

UK TERMS		SYMBOL	US TERMS	
Stitch	St		Stitch	St
Chain	CH	⬭	Chain	CH
Slip stitch	Sl St	●	Slip stitch	Sl St
Double crochet	DC	+	Single crochet	SC
Half treble	HTR	T	Half double	HDC
Treble	TR	T	Double crochet	DC
Cluster (treble 3)	CL	⩔	Cluster (double crochet 3)	CL
Double treble	DTR	T	Treble	TR
Treble 2 together	TR2TOG	⋀	Double treble 2 together	DTR2TOG
Double treble 3 together	DTR3TOG	⧖	Triple treble 3 together	TRTR3TOG

Terms and techniques

ADDING/JOINING IN YARN – Sometimes when working you will run out of yarn, or your yarn will have a join mid row/round. This means you will need to join in a new strand of yarn. If your yarn has a knot in it that you do not trust to hold (I never trust them), snip the knot out, leave at least 8cm (3¼in) of your existing yarn to sew in, and leave an 8cm (3¼in) tail on your new yarn. Pinch these tails together and work the next stitch or tie them with a knot. You can then either work over the ends or sew them in to secure them.

BLOCKING – Flattening, neatening and evening out finished crochet motifs or fabric through the process of pinning them out to the desired shape and size and dampening or steaming them, then leaving them to dry.

BORDER – Adding an edging to crochet motifs or finished pieces to extend, decorate or neaten the edges of the work.

(BRACKETS) – Stitches together in brackets are to be worked into the same stitch or space.

CHAIN SPACE – The space created by chain stitching between sets of stitches. Sometimes a pattern will call for working into a chain space.

CHANGING COLOUR – I prefer to secure my yarn when changing colour: fasten off the old colour and join in the new colour with a slip stitch. If you're changing colours when working the square motifs in this book, start the new colour in a different corner each time to spread out your yarn ends. This will prevent one section of your design feeling bulky when you sew in the yarn tails at the end.

CLUSTER(S) – No fixed definition. This term is an abbreviation for a group of stitches, but the exact make-up of the group can vary. In this book a cluster refers to a group of 3 trebles worked into the same stitch or space/gap.

CROCHET IN YARN ENDS – On some motifs it is possible to crochet over the yarn ends as the work progresses. This reduces the number of ends that need to be woven in when the project is completed.

DECREASE – Reduce the number of stitches by working several stitches together.

EASE – The difference between the measurements of the garment and the measurements of the intended wearer.

FASTEN OFF – Finishing off the last stitch securely so that it stops the work from unravelling.

FOUNDATION CHAIN – A foundation chain is a length of chain stitches that starts a project off.

FOUNDATION RING – The first set of chain stitches, which, when joined together form the foundation for the first round of crochet.

INCREASE – Increasing the number of stitches by working more than one stitch in the same place.

METERAGE/YARDAGE – The number of metres/yards of yarn used. Yarn meterage/yardage is given on the yarn ball band.

RIGHT SIDE – The side of the crochet that will be on show once completed.

ROUND – A round of crochet worked around a central starting point or piece edge and joined together in the place where you started.

ROW – A row of crochet is worked in a line along an edge and the rows are worked back and forth.

SCHEMATIC – A chart of symbols representing stitches that illustrate a pattern. Use the stitch key in the Stitches and Terms chart see opposite for reference. To read a schematic, follow the diagram working from the centre outwards, round by round. The schematics are designed for right-handed working, which means they are read anticlockwise; however, if you're left-handed you should follow the stitches in a clockwise direction.

SLIP KNOT – The knot used to create the first loop on the crochet hook that acts as the first chain.

SPACE – Gap between stitches.

TENSION/GAUGE – The number of stitches and rows made over a set area. It's crucial to know tension for garments because it's important to achieve the correct size; however, for blankets the exact tension may not be so vital.

TOTAL STITCHES – Can refer to any stitch. Used to show the total number of stitches in a round or row. Usually shown in brackets on pattern instructions

TURN – Reverse the motif/fabric you're working on.

WEAVE IN ENDS – After fastening off, weave any ends of yarn into the motif/main fabric so that they cannot be seen. This can be done with a yarn needle or latch tool, and it is recommended that you weave in as you complete each motif to save a mammoth task at the end.

WORKING INTO THE BACK OF THE STITCH – Working a stitch into the top, back strand/bar of stitch (single strand).

WORKING INTO THE STITCH – Working a stitch into both strands/bars of the top of the stitch.

WORKING INTO THE SPACE/GAP – Working into the space or gap between the stitches.

WRONG SIDE – The side of the motif/fabric which will not be seen when the item is completed.

YARN ROUND HOOK – Wind the yarn around the hook.

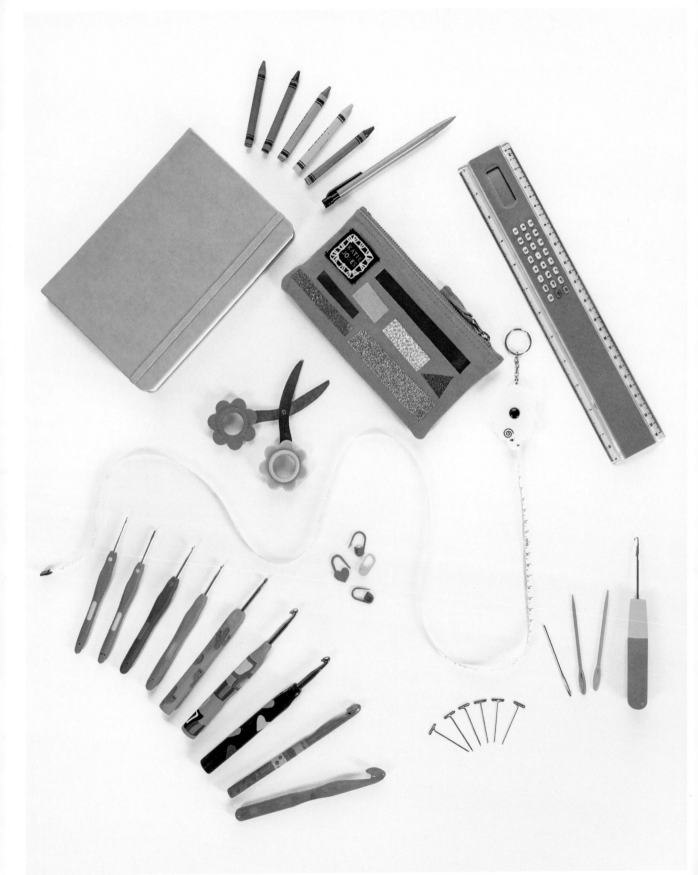

TOOLS

One of the main advantages of crochet is that so little equipment is required to start to enjoy the craft. This makes it an inexpensive craft to embark on and very portable.

The Essentials

Though you only need a hook, yarn and scissors to get started crocheting, the tools listed here will help you to create the projects in this book.

TYPES OF HOOK
Hooks can be made from many materials including metal, bamboo, plastic and wood. They can have straight handles or shaped plastic grips, which some people find more comfortable to hold and work with. The type of hook you use is a matter of personal choice.

HOOK SIZES
Hooks come in a range of sizes from 2mm to 10mm or even larger. They go up in half sizes and the size of the hook is usually stamped on the handle. Most crochet worked in DK (light worsted), aran (worsted) or chunky (bulky) yarn is done on hooks ranging from 3mm to 7mm.

STITCH MARKERS
These are usually made of brightly coloured plastic or metal and shaped like small safety pins. They are used to mark a specific row or stitch where needed.

TAPE MEASURE
Essential for measuring pattern sizing, checking crochet tension and final sizes of pieces.

SMALL SCISSORS/YARN NIPPERS
To cut yarn cleanly and snip yarn ends after weaving in.

YARN/TAPESTRY NEEDLES
Large-eyed plastic or metal needles which are used to sew crochet together and to weave in finished ends.

DIGITAL SCALES (KITCHEN SCALES)
Use to calculate the amount of yarn needed for each piece by weighing a motif and multiplying the results.

NOTEBOOK/SQUARED PAPER
To note any changes to a pattern (e.g., different hook size) and draw out your designs.

CALCULATOR
To calculate the amount of yarn required for the finished piece. For example, multiplying the amount of yarn used in one motif.

Other Useful Equipment

LARGE-HEADED PINS
For use when blocking out motifs or garments.

STEAM IRON/WATER SPRAY
For dampening the pieces when blocking out.

IRONING BOARD/CHILDREN'S FOAM PLAY MAT
For pinning out pieces when blocking out.

CRAYONS/COLOURED PENS
To plan the colours to be used in your pieces.

LATCH HOOK
A latch hook can be used as an alternative to a needle when weaving in ends.

YARNS

When it comes to yarn, the choice is almost endless!

The term yarn is the general name for a strand of fibres that can be crocheted or knitted. There are many different yarns available: you can choose from different textures and fibre types and different colours and weights. Yarn can be constructed in different ways and from different materials. Some yarn is derived from natural sources, some man-made and some recycled. All have different properties that will generate different results.

YARN WEIGHTS AND RECOMMENDED HOOK SIZES

This table shows the different yarn weights available and their recommended hook size ranges. A heavier weight means a thicker yarn. The information on what yarn type (weight) and recommended hook to use is also often printed on the yarn label.

2 FINE	3 LIGHT	4 MEDIUM	5 BULKY	6 SUPER BULKY / 7 JUMBO
Baby Sport 2/3/4 ply	Double Knit DK (Light Worsted)	Aran Worsted	Chunky (Bulky)	Super Chunky Jumbo
Hooks 2.5-3.5 mm	Hooks 3-4.5 mm	Hooks 4.5-6.5 mm	Hooks 6-9 mm	Hooks 9-20mm

It's great to visit a yarn store to get up close and personal with the options, and to see the ranges available. Understanding how a fibre feels is important, especially for wearable garments. The main two yarn groups are natural and synthetic; however, you can also get blends of the two.

- **Popular natural yarn fibres:**
  wool, silk, linen and cotton.

- **Popular synthetic yarn fibres:**
  acrylic, viscose, nylon and polyamide.

Some fibres, like wool, and fluffy fibres that trap the heat, are more suited to wearing in cooler months. Fibres like cotton have better cooling properties and can be worn in warmer weather. When producing a project, especially a large design, using a synthetic yarn or a blend may be optimal due to its cost and durability. In this book I have created projects that use easily obtainable yarns in the most popular weights. The projects give the weight and the tension, but picking the yarn fibre, brand or colourway is your own individual design choice.

Yarn is sold according to total weight and not length. Different yarns of the same style can have varying lengths even if they are the same weight. Because these factors vary from brand to brand, the patterns in this book state the meterage to show approximate yarn quantities for the projects. More details on the yarn brands used to produce the projects in this book can be found on page 176.

GETTING YOUR GRIP

Getting your hand grip right and working out how best to maintain an even tension can be the trickiest part of starting to crochet. Practice really does make perfect; don't let it defeat you.

Holding your hands in a crochet hook grip can feel odd at first, but with a little practice the action should soon kick into autopilot. If you are new to crochet, practising your grip just by doing the chain stitch is my main recommendation. Put on your favourite tunes and keep chaining till you find your rhythm!

PENCIL HOLD

KNIFE HOLD

Holding the Hook

Rule number one is that there are no fixed rules! There is no right or wrong way to hold your hook. You should hold the hook in your dominant hand, and it needs to feel comfortable to you. Left are the two most popular holds.

Holding the Yarn

Your non-dominant hand does what I think is all the hard work in crochet and getting your yarn hold right and feeling comfortable can take a little practice. Again, there are no set rules, but finding a way to keep your tension smooth is important. My top tip is to try to hold your hand in such a way that you have an 'antenna' finger, this helps with keeping smooth tension (see page 27).

Getting your grip sorted will help the smoothness of stitching and the flow of your work. Grab your hook and some yarn to match its size – starting off with a chunky yarn will help with mastering your hand hold before trying new stitches.

My favourite, go-to hold that I swear by is the 'shadow puppet bunny'. This may sound like a silly name but it's a good way to remember the hand positioning.

Shadow Puppet Bunny Hold:

1   To set your hand up in this formation, either loop the yarn around your little finger or pinch it there to help keep tension.

2   The yarn then loops from the inside of your hand to over the top of your fingers.

3   Hold your hand in a shadow puppet bunny shape using either your thumb and your fore finger or middle finger (bunny mouth). Where your fingers meet, pinch the yarn and hold the working yarn close to the hook. Your middle finger or forefinger (the bunny ear) then works as your 'antenna' which keeps an area of yarn smooth, for tension.

4   The area between your pinch and 'antenna' is where you hook the yarn to create the stitch. By circling your hook and working over the yarn in this area, the yarn catches on the hook and is easy to pull through a stitch without dropping off.

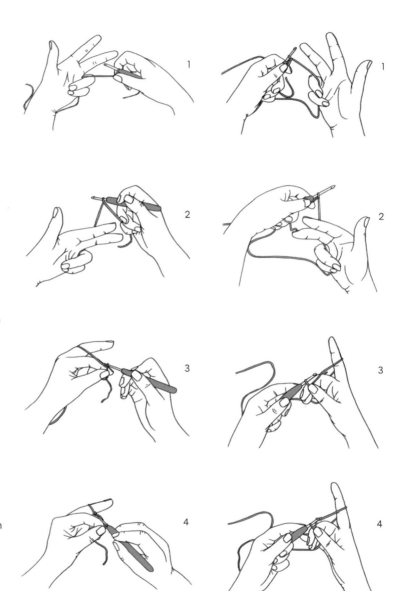

GUIDE TO STITCHES

Now you have got your grip, let's get to know all the basic stitches!

This illustrated guide takes you step by step through all the stitches you will need to whip up your motif squares and project makes. Just remember the stitches are given in UK terms in this book.

If you are new to crochet, I recommend grabbing a hook and some yarn and giving some of these stitches a go before starting your first project!

If you are right handed you will work your crochet anti-clockwise and if you are left handed you will work clockwise.

Slip Knot

This is the knot that becomes the first loop on your hook, this knot is counted as a stitch. When starting you should leave a yarn tail that is long enough to weave in at the end.

1   Make a loop with the yarn. Insert the hook through the middle of the loop, hook the yarn and pull it through.

2   This is your slip knot. The loop is adjustable, pull it so that it is snug but not too tight, against the hook.

1   2

Chain Stitch

This is a single stitch that can be worked consecutively to form a chain. All stitches start with the slip knot on the hook.

1   To begin your first chain, wrap the yarn around the hook anticlockwise (clockwise if left-handed).

2   Catch the yarn with the hook and pull the yarn through the slip knot on the hook.

3   This is your first chain stitch – only when a stitch is off the hook does it count as a stitch. Make the next chain by wrapping the yarn around the hook and pulling it through the loop on the hook again. Continue to produce the required number of chain stitches.

4   As you work, hold the chain being created with your non-dominant hand near the hook to control the tension. You will need to reposition your hand every few stitches to ensure you keep an even tension.

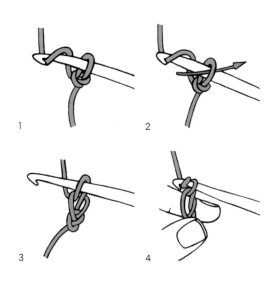

Anatomy of a Chain

A crochet chain has a front and back. The front looks like a series of 'v' shapes, on the back is a series of bumps. Each v shape or bump equals one chain.

FRONT OF CHAIN

BACK OF CHAIN

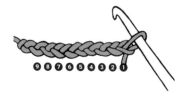

Slip Stitch

Slip stitches have no height and are used as joining stitches and in places where you need to move along a row or round.

1   Insert the hook into the next stitch.

2   Wrap the yarn around the hook and pull it through not only the stitch but also the first loop on the hook.

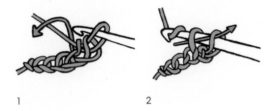

1   2

Foundation Ring

This method forms a ring into which you can begin crocheting your first round.

1   Make a chain with the number of stitches specified in the pattern.

2   Close the ring by inserting the hook into the first chain and working a slip stitch by pulling the yarn through both loops.

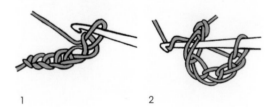

1   2

Double Crochet

Double crochet stitches are simple, compact stitches that form a dense fabric and are often used in edgings and toy making. They can also be used for joining two pieces of fabric (see page 63).

1   Insert the hook into the stitch or space. Wrap the yarn around the hook and pull the yarn through to the front.

2   You should have two loops on your hook. Wrap the yarn around the hook.

3   Pull the yarn through both loops. There should be one loop left on your hook. You have created a double crochet.

Half Treble

A stitch that's halfway between a double crochet and a treble in height and looks slightly looser than a double crochet. Often used when shaping edges and in motifs.

1   Wrap the yarn around the hook and insert the hook into the stitch or space. Wrap the yarn around the hook and pull the yarn through to the front.

2   You should now have three loops on your hook. Wrap the yarn around the hook and pull through all three loops, leaving one loop on your hook.

3   You have created a half treble crochet.

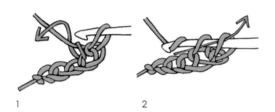

1   2

3

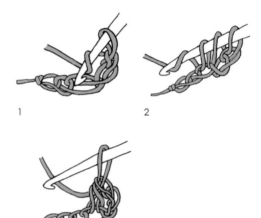

1   2

3

Treble Crochet

This is probably the most popular crochet stitch for use in Granny Squares. It is twice the height of a double crochet stitch.

1   Wrap the yarn around the hook and insert the hook into the stitch or space. Wrap the yarn round the hook and pull the yarn through to the front.

2   You should have three loops on your hook. Wrap the yarn around the hook and pull through two loops.

3   You should have two loops on your hook. Wrap the yarn around the hook and pull through the final two loops, leaving one loop on your hook.

4   You have created a treble crochet.

Double Treble Crochet

This is worked in the same way as a treble crochet stitch, but the yarn is wrapped around the hook twice to start.

1   Wrap the yarn around the hook twice. Insert the hook into the stitch or space. Wrap the yarn round the hook and pull the yarn through to the front.

2   You should have four loops on your hook. Wrap the yarn around the hook and pull the yarn through the first two loops.

3   You should have three loops on your hook. Wrap the yarn around the hook and pull the yarn through the next two loops.

4   Two loops on your hook. Wrap the yarn around the hook and pull it through the final two loops.

5   One loop left on the hook. This completes the double treble crochet.

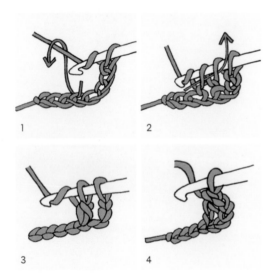

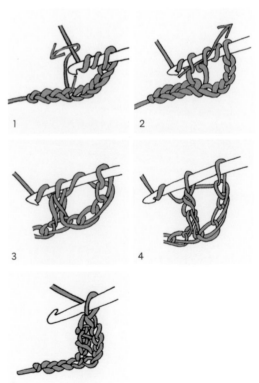

Trebling or Double Trebling Together

This technique involves working trebles together and is done by leaving the last step of the stitch on the hook when you begin the next stitch. Repeat this process for the number and type of stitches given in the pattern, and then pull the yarn through all the loops on your hook for the final step. This is one way to reduce the number of stitches or to create petal shapes.

To work the double treble 3 together to form the petals on the flower motif:

1   Wrap the yarn around hook twice.

2   Insert the hook into the stitch.

3   Wrap the yarn around the hook.

4   Pull the yarn through to the front, you should have four loops on your hook.

5   Wrap the yarn around the hook.

6   Pull the first 2 loops through, leaving 3 loops on your hook.

7   Wrap the yarn around the hook.

8   Pull the next two loops through, leaving two loops on your hook.

9   Repeat steps 1–8 twice more.

10 Wrap the yarn around the hook.

11 Pull the yarn through all four loops on your hook.

12 Leaving 1 loop on your hook. This creates the double treble 3 together.

WORKING IN DIFFERENT STITCHES TO REDUCE/DECREASE

WORKING IN DIFFERENT STITCHES TO CREATE A PETAL

Working Stitches into a Foundation Ring

The square motifs in this book all start with a foundation ring and the stitches of the first round are worked by inserting the hook into the centre of the ring. Turning chains are used to get to the right height for the stitches of your first round. If you work over the yarn tail as you stitch into the foundation ring for the first round, you can pull the tail to close up your central hole - if you wish to.

Turning Chains

If you're crocheting in rows or rounds you will need to add turning chains at the beginning of each row/round. This acts as a fake first stitch of the row/round, and is used to bring the hook up to the height of the stitches you are crocheting. Each basic stitch has its own number of chains. For double crochet this is 1 chain, for half trebles 2 chains, for trebles 3 chains and for double trebles 4 chains. If wanting to count the total number of stitches in a row or round - remember to include your turning chain fake stitch in this.

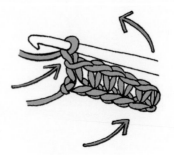

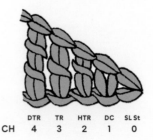

CH	DTR 4	TR 3	HTR 2	DC 1	SL St 0

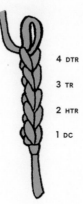

4 DTR

3 TR

2 HTR

1 DC

Fastening Off

Finish with a slip stitch join or final stitch.

1   Make one chain.

2   Cut the yarn, leaving at least 8–10cm (4in) yarn tail (or more if specified in the pattern).

3   Pull the cut yarn through the loop of the chain and pull tightly so that the fabric does not unravel.

TENSION

One of the most important aspects of mastering crochet is understanding tension. Tension refers to the number of stitches and rounds or rows that fit into a square of crochet fabric of a specific size.

Tension can be determined by the size of your hook and the weight of your yarn, but it can also vary a lot from person to person depending on how you hold your hook and yarn or even on your mood at the time! If you are new to crochet, get some practice before diving into your first project so that you can develop your working rhythm and get an even tension.

Finding an Even Tension

Getting an even tension can feel difficult at first, but practice makes perfect. Although it might seem boring, keep practising chain stitch until you find your rhythm because this will make the next steps and learning the next stitches so much easier.

Once you have found your rhythm and your stitches are even, try matching the specified yarn weight and hook size to the tension measurements on one of the projects in this book. Because all the projects are made from square blocks, the tension guides for each project are given for the size of one whole motif. If your measurements don't match up at first, don't worry, crochet tension can really vary, just remember it's a lot easier to change your hook size than try to change yourself. If your tension comes out too small try going up a hook size and if your tension comes out too large, try sizing down. Play around with hook sizes till your motif matches up with the measurements.

Tension Sample

The importance of producing a tension sample for garments cannot be overstated. Because the garments are made from squares, small differences in your square sizes when multiplied can make a big difference to the overall size of your piece, so it can be useful to have hooks in a range of sizes.

For some homewares and accessories, such as blankets or bags, exact sizing may not be too important, but it is useful to understand your tension.

When measuring your tension square lay it out flat, but do not over stretch it; you may want to pin it out on a blocking mat to hold it square. Use a tape measure or ruler to measure across the square to get your tension measurement.

THE SQUARES

INTRODUCING THE FIVE SQUARES!

GO GET YOUR SQUARE ON!

1 GRANNY
2 BLOCK
3 SPOT
4 FLOWER
5 FERRIS WHEEL

Grab a hook and some yarn and begin practising your squares.

Use the stitch guide on pages 20-26 for full stitch instructions. I recommend making all the squares before you begin your projects to see which ones you prefer. It's a great way to practise your stitches, play with colour combinations and see the type of fabric that each square design produces.

In the pattern instructions the yarn colour is changed for each round. It's a good idea to start off changing colour every round because it makes it easier to see each round and your individual stitches; however, once you have the knack of stitching squares, you might prefer to make some one-colour squares or vary how many rounds you have in one colour.

GRANNY SQUARE

A firm favourite and the original classic square, say hello to the traditional Granny. This is where my love of the crochet square started and is our first motif! This pattern is worked over four rounds with the stitches worked into the gaps. The Granny Square is a timeless classic and the most famous of all the squares. Its repeating rounds also make it an easy design to extend into a larger motif.

Top Tips

WORKING IN ONE COLOUR

To work the Granny Square or any continuing rounds in the same colour replace steps A, B and C of rounds 2, 3 and 4 with:

Slip stitch into the next chain space, chain 5.

Continue following the rest of the instructions for the round; omit fastening off if you wish to continue in the same colour.

INCREASING THE SIZE OF YOUR SQUARE

To increase the size of your Granny Square simply repeat round 4, replacing steps E and H with:

Work 1 cluster into each gap up to the corner chain space.

GRANNY SQUARE PATTERN

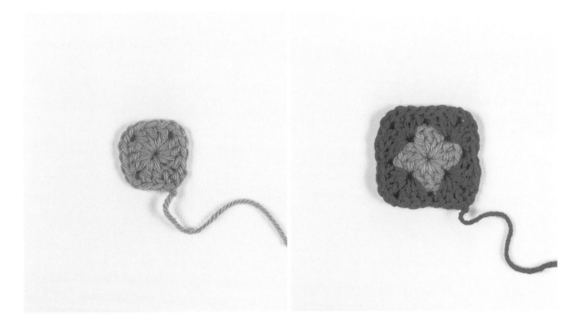

FOUNDATION

A   Using your first colour, chain 4 stitches.
B   Slip stitch into the first chain to form your
    foundation ring.

ROUND 1

A   To begin your first round, chain 5 stitches.
    The first 3 chains of this work as a fake treble
    and the next 2 are the first corner. You need
    chains at the start to get the right stitch
    height at the centre of your work.
B   Work 3 trebles into the centre of the ring.
C   To complete your first round, (chain 2, treble 3)
    into the ring twice.
D   Chain 2, treble 2, join with a slip stitch into
    the third chain at the start of the round to
    complete the round. The first chain, which
    creates the fake treble, and the final 2 trebles
    form the final cluster. For future rounds,
    3 trebles will be known as one cluster.
E   To fasten off your round, create an extra chain,
    cut your yarn leaving at least 8–10 cm (3¼–4 in)
    and pull through the loop to secure.

ROUND 2

A   Start with the next colour on your hook.
B   Join in with a slip stitch at any chain space.
C   Chain 5 stitches.
D   Work your first cluster into the same space
    where you joined in.
E   (Cluster, chain 2, cluster) in the following three
    corner chain spaces.
F   Treble 2 into the first chain space.
G   Join with a slip stitch into the third chain at
    the start of the round to complete the round.
H   Fasten off.

Tip: Joining in new colours at different corners for
each new round helps distribute where the loose
yarn ends are in your squares and this helps with
sewing the ends in neatly when finishing a square.

ROUND 3

A Start with the next colour on your hook.
B Join in with a slip stitch at any chain space.
C Chain 5 stitches.
D Work your first cluster into the same space where you joined in.
E Working into the space between clusters, work one cluster.
F (Cluster, chain 2, cluster) into the corner chain space.
G Repeat steps E and F twice more.
H Work one cluster into the space.
I Treble 2 into the first chain space.
J Join with a slip stitch into the third chain at the start of the round to complete the round.
K Fasten off.

ROUND 4

A Start with the next colour on your hook.
B Join in with a slip stitch at any corner chain space.
C Chain 5 stitches.
D Work your first cluster into the same space where you joined in.
E Work clusters into the next two spaces between clusters.
F (Cluster, chain 2, cluster) into the corner chain space.
G Repeat steps E and F twice more.
H Work clusters into the next two spaces between clusters.
I Treble 2 into the first chain space.
J Join with a slip stitch into the third chain at the start of the round to complete the round.
K Fasten off.

BLOCK SQUARE

The Block Square is the Granny Square's less lacy counterpart. This square is perfect for making a more solid fabric and is easy to extend into a larger motif. This is a four-round design, and the stitches are worked into the gaps between one another. My top tip for this square is that when you change colours try to crochet over the previous round's tail to reduce how many ends you must sew in.

Top Tips

WORKING IN ONE COLOUR

To work the square or any continuing rounds in the same colour replace steps A, B and C of rounds 2, 3 and 4 with:

Slip stitch into the chain space, chain 5.

Continue following the rest of the round instructions; omit fastening off round if you wish to continue in the same colour.

INCREASING THE SIZE OF YOUR SQUARE

To increase the size of your Block Square, simply repeat round 4, replacing steps E and H with:

Work trebles in the gaps between the stitches up to the corner chain space.

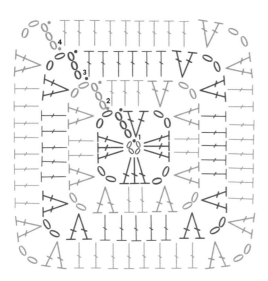

BLOCK SQUARE PATTERN

FOUNDATION

A   Using the first colour, chain 4 stitches.
B   Slip stitch into the first chain to form your foundation ring.

ROUND 1

A   To begin round 1, chain 5 stitches. The first 3 chains work as a fake treble and chains 4 and 5 form the first corner. It's necessary to chain at the start of the round to get the required stitch height.
B   Work 3 trebles into the centre of the ring.
C   To complete your first round (chain 2, treble 3) into the ring twice.
D   Chain 2, treble 2, join with a slip stitch into the third chain at the start of the round to complete the round. The first chain, which worked as the fake treble, and the final 2 trebles form the final cluster.
E   To fasten off, create an extra chain, cut your yarn leaving at least 8–10 cm (3¼–4 in) and pull through the loop to secure.

ROUND 2

A   Start with the next colour on your hook.
B   Join in with a slip stitch at any corner chain space.
C   Chain 5 stitches.
D   Work 2 trebles into the space where you joined in.
E   Work trebles in the gaps between the next 2 stitches.
F   (Treble 2, chain 2, treble 2) in the corner chain space.
G   Repeat steps E–F twice more.
H   Work trebles in the gaps between the next 2 stitches.
I   Work a treble into the chain space where you began the round.
J   Join with a slip stitch into the third chain at the start of the round to complete the round.
K   Fasten off.

Tip: Joining in new colours at different corners for each new round helps distribute where the loose yarn ends are in your squares.

ROUND 3

A   Start with the next colour on your hook.
B   Join in with a slip stitch at any corner chain space.
C   Chain 5 stitches.
D   Work 2 trebles into the space where you joined in.
E   Work trebles in the gaps between the next 5 stitches.
F   (Treble 2, chain 2, treble 2) in the corner chain space.
G   Repeat steps E–F twice more.
H   Work trebles in the gaps between the next 5 stitches.
I   Work a treble into the chain space where you began the round.
J   Join with a slip stitch into the third chain at the start of the round to complete the round.
K   Fasten off.

ROUND 4

A   Start with the next colour on your hook.
B   Join in with a slip stitch at any corner chain space.
C   Chain 5 stitches.
D   Work 2 trebles into the space where you joined in.
E   Work trebles in the gaps between the next 8 stitches, up to the corner chain space.
F   (Treble 2, chain 2, treble 2) in the corner chain space.
G   Repeat steps E–F twice more.
H   Work trebles in the gaps between the next 8 stitches, up to the corner chain space.
I   Work a treble into the chain space where you began the round.
J   Join with a slip stitch into the third chain at the start of the round to complete the round.
K   Fasten off.

SPOT SQUARE

The Spot Square is a graphic take on the Granny Square. You can easily change the look of the design by mixing the colours: a simple switch can take the look from polka dots to target stripes. This design starts out as a circle which is then squared off in the final round. This is a four-round design where the stitches are worked into the top of the stitches on the previous round.

Top Tips

WORKING IN ONE COLOUR

To work the Spot Square in one colour, skip step A and replace step B in Rounds 2 and 3 with:

Slip stitch into next stitch.

Continue following the rest of the instructions for the round; omit fastening off if you wish to continue in the same colour.

INCREASING THE SIZE OF YOUR SQUARE

To increase the size of your square, simply follow the Granny Square increase instructions on page 33.

SPOT SQUARE PATTERN

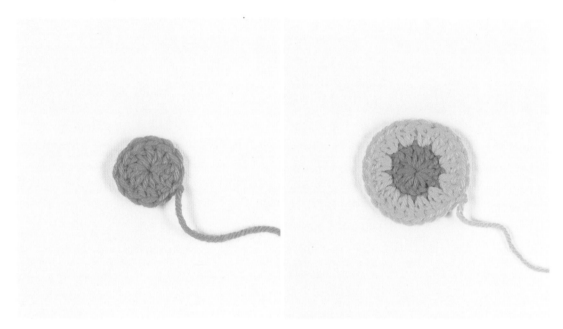

FOUNDATION

A   Using the first colour, chain 3 stitches.
B   Slip stitch into the first chain to form
    your foundation ring.

ROUND 1

A   Chain 3, this becomes a fake treble.
B   Work 11 treble stitches into the centre of the
    loop. Try to work over the beginning tail as it
    can be pulled like a drawstring to make the
    centre point tight.
C   Join with a slip stitch into the third chain at
    the start of the round to complete the round.
D   To fasten off create an extra chain, cut your
    yarn leaving at least 8-10cm (3¼–4in) and
    pull through the loop to secure.

ROUND 2

A   Start with the next colour on your hook.
B   Join in with a slip stitch where you fastened
    off in round 1.
C   Chain 3.
D   Treble into same stitch where you joined in.
E   Work 2 trebles into the top of each stitch
    of the round.
F   Join with a slip stitch into the third chain
    at the start of the round to complete the
    round. Total of 24 stitches.
G   Fasten off.

ROUND 3

A   Start with the next colour on your hook.
B   Join in with a slip stitch where you fastened off in round 2.
C   Chain 3.
D   Treble into the same stitch where you joined in.
E   Treble into the top of the next stitch.
F   Work 2 trebles into the top of the next stitch.
G   Repeat steps E and F until you have worked into every stitch of round 2.
H   Join with a slip stitch into the third chain at the start of the round to complete the round.
I   Fasten off.

ROUND 4

A   Start with the next colour on your hook.
B   Join in with a slip stitch on any stitch.
C   Chain 6 stitches to make your first fake double treble and your 2 corner chains.
D   Working into the same stitch where you joined in, work 3 double trebles.
E   Miss 2 stitches.
F   Work 3 trebles into the next stitch.
G   Repeat steps E and F.
H   Miss 2 stitches.
I   (Double treble 3, chain 2, double treble 3) in the next stitch.
J   Repeat steps E to I, twice more.
K   Repeat steps E to G.
L   Miss 2 stitches.
M   Double treble 2 into the first stitch where you joined in.
N   Join with a slip stitch into the fourth chain at the start of the round to complete the round.
O   Fasten off.

FLOWER SQUARE

Flower Power! This floral twist on the Granny Square packs a summery punch. The motif uses double treble stitches worked together to form its petals and is worked in a circle, which is squared off in the last round. The stitches in this design are worked into both the top of the stitch and the gaps. This pattern is the only three-round design in the book, but due to its tall petal stitches, it ends up the same size as its four-round counterparts.

Top Tips

WORKING IN ONE COLOUR

To work the Flower Square in one colour, replace steps A and B from Rounds 2 and 3 with:

Round 2: *Slip stitch into next stitch.*

Round 3: *Slip stitch into chain space.*

Continue following the rest of the round instructions, omit fastening off if you wish to continue in the same colour.

INCREASING THE SIZE OF YOUR SQUARE

To increase the size of your square, simply follow the Granny Square increase instructions on page 33.

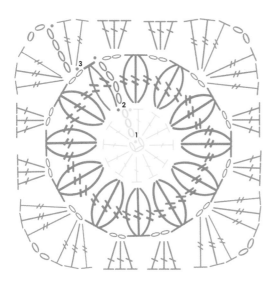

FLOWER SQUARE PATTERN

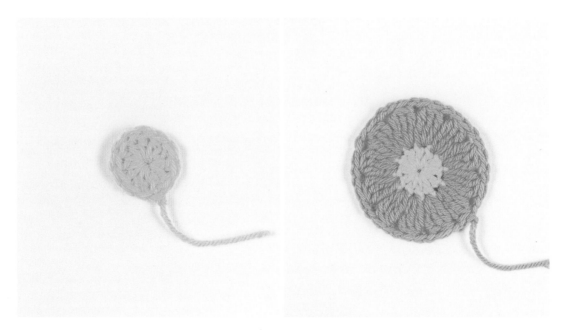

FOUNDATION

A Using your first colour, chain 3 stitches.
B Slip stitch into the first chain to form your foundation ring.

ROUND 1

A Chain 3 to make your first fake treble.
B Work 11 treble stitches into the centre of the loop. Try to work over the beginning tail so it can be pulled like a drawstring to make the centre point tight.
C Join with a slip stitch into the third chain at the start of the round to complete the round. (12 stitches in total).
D To fasten off create an extra chain, cut your yarn leaving at least 8-10cm (3¼-4in) and pull through the loop to secure.

ROUND 2

A Start with the next colour on your hook.
B Join in with a slip stitch in any stitch.
C Chain 4 stitches to make your first fake double treble.
D Working into the same stitch where you joined in, double treble 2 stitches together.
E Chain 2 stitches.
F Working into the next stitch, double treble 3 stitches together. This creates one petal.
G Repeat steps E and F in every stitch of the round until you have 12 petals.
H Chain 2 stitches.
I Join into the top of the first double treble with a slip stitch to complete the round.
J Fasten off.

Tension note: If the chains between the petals feel too tight you could increase to 3 chains between each petal instead of 2.

This pattern is the only three-round design in the book, but due to its tall petal stitches, it ends up the same size as its four-round counterparts.

ROUND 3

A   Start with the next colour on your hook.

B   Join in with a slip stitch in any chain space.

C   Chain 6 stitches to make your first fake double treble and 2 corner chains.

D   Working into the same space where you joined in, work 3 double trebles.

E   Work 3 trebles into the next 2 chain spaces.

F   In the next chain space, (double treble 3, chain 2, double treble 3).

G   Repeat steps D–E, twice more.

H   Work 3 trebles into the next 2 chain spaces.

I   Work 2 double trebles into the chain space where you first joined in.

J   Join with a slip stitch into the fourth chain at the start of the round to complete the round.

K   Fasten off.

FERRIS WHEEL SQUARE

The Ferris Wheel Square is a variation on the traditional Granny, mixing patterns and stitch types to create an intricate design. Inspired by decorative tiles, this pattern is a four-round design where the stitches are worked into the gaps. Changing the colours of your rows can really change the look of this design: by using the same colour for rounds three and four you can make the centre of the design pop so that it looks like a small flower motif.

Top Tips

WORKING IN ONE COLOUR

To work the Ferris Wheel Square or any continuing rounds in the same colour, replace steps A and B from Rounds 2, 3 and 4 with:

Slip Stitch into the next space.

Continue following the rest of the round instructions; omit fastening off if you wish to continue in the same colour.

INCREASING THE SIZE OF YOUR SQUARE

To increase the size of your square simply follow the Block Square increase instructions on page 37.

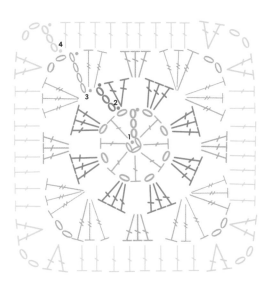

FERRIS WHEEL PATTERN

FOUNDATION

A   With the first colour chain 3 stitches.
B   Slip stitch into the first chain to form
    your foundation ring.

ROUND 1

A   To begin round 1, chain 4 stitches. The first
    3 chains work as a fake treble and the fourth
    chain is a space stitch. It's necessary to chain
    at the start of the round to get the required
    stitch height.
B   Work 1 treble into the centre of the ring,
    followed by 1 chain.
C   Repeat step B until you have 8 trebles
    (7 trebles and 1 fake treble).
D   Join with a slip stitch into the third chain at
    the start of the round to complete the round.
E   To fasten off create an extra chain, cut your
    yarn leaving at least 8-10 cm (3¼-4 in) and
    pull through the loop to secure.

ROUND 2

A   Start with the next colour on your hook.
B   Join in with a slip stitch in any chain space.
C   Chain 3 stitches.
D   Work 3 trebles into the next chain space.
E   Work 3 trebles into each chain space
    of the round. From now on, 3 trebles
    in a space will be known as a cluster.
F   Work 2 trebles in the first chain space
    to complete the first cluster.
G   Join with a slip stitch into the third chain
    at the start of the round to complete
    the round.
H   Fasten off.

ROUND 3

A Start with the next colour on your hook.
B Join in at any gap between clusters.
C Chain 6 stitches.
D Work 3 double trebles into the same space where you joined in.
E Work one cluster into the next space between clusters.
F Working into the next space between clusters (double treble 3, chain 2, double treble 3).
G Repeat steps E and F once more.
H Work one cluster into the next space between clusters.
I Double treble 2 into the first chain space.
J Join with a slip stitch into the fourth chain at the start of the round.
K Fasten off.

ROUND 4

A Start with the next colour on your hook.
B Join in with a slip stitch in any corner chain space.
C Chain 5 stitches.
D Work 2 trebles into the same space where you joined in.
E Treble in-between each stitch up to the corner chain space.
F (Treble 2, chain 2, treble 2) into the corner chain space.
G Repeat steps E–F twice more.
H Treble in-between each stitch up to the corner chain space.
I Treble into the first chain space where you began.
J Join with a slip stitch into the third chain at the start of the round.
K Fasten off.

DESIGN AND MAKE

CUSTOMISING AND CALCULATING DESIGNS

This book aims to provide you with some great techniques, tips and tricks to follow. You are free to follow the designs exactly or you can switch them up and swap them about as much as you like, mixing and matching and customising to your heart's content! Making pieces yourself is all about creating your makes, your way – adding your own personality and style and getting the perfect fit for you or your home!

Starting from the five square motif patterns your options for customising the projects are almost endless. You can change the feel and look of a square drastically just by changing the weight of yarn you choose or how many colours you include. The variations you can create grow exponentially when you consider changing or switching the squares in a design. Swatching and planning is an essential part of the design process to help work out your ideas before undergoing the, sometimes lengthy, process of making. Crochet is a labour of love, fully working out what you want to make before you start helps keep that love alive!

Yarn Choice

Yarn comes in all shapes and sizes; even within yarn classifications, such as DK (light worsted), there can be quite a range of actual thicknesses between different brands and fibre types. Different yarns will have different weights and bodies, which can affect how a project feels or drapes. Switching yarns can create big differences

and bring a whole new feeling to a pattern. Do you want a cool, crisp cotton or a fluffy wool? Making these decisions will really affect the feel of your project. That's why swatching with different yarns and creating a tension square is so vital. It gives you an idea of the feel and drape of your yarn and allows you to make sure it meets the project's tension requirements.

Bearing all this in mind, I didn't want to be too prescriptive when it came to the exact yarn types for each project, so I have only listed the yarn weight to meet the tension for each design; however, if you want more detailed information on the yarns used, please see page 176.

Colour

If you hadn't guessed it already, colour is very important to me. I LOVE IT, and I like to use a lot of it. The great thing about the patterns in this book is that you may love them and want to use the same colours or you might love naturals and neutrals – making your own pieces means you get to decide what colours to use!

One of my top tips for picking colours is creating a mood board. You may want to use Pinterest or, like me, start a sketchbook where you can play with images and colour palettes. I recommend collecting paint swatches from a DIY store – these are great to play with when you're working out ideas. I like to punch holes in them and start matching yarns to them. Keep some of your snipped ends for this. The more yarns you use the bigger your colour library will become.

I also like looking at the work of artists for inspiration on what colours work well together. A couple of go-tos for the projects in this book were Yayoi Kusama, Niki de Saint Phalle and Camille Walala.

And my final top tip: if you're making something for you or your home, look around you. If you're making a garment, dive into your wardrobe – what pieces do you love? What would you wear with the piece you're making? Pick and choose colours that match or complement your favourite items. The same rules apply for your home.

Planning Your Project

When using this book you may wish to use the designs as patterns to follow or the shapes as templates to fill, either way, planning your project is a really important step. Sketching and swatching are great ways to work out yarn types, your tension and colourways. You don't need to be Michelangelo, just using some squared paper will do most of the work for you! Drawing out your design is a useful way to begin picturing your piece, it's also a lot easier to play around with colours and patterns this way than with trial and error. I always love to draw out and colour in a range of different colourways and select my favourite before swatching!

Plan out your projects using the total number of squares. This number is provided in either the materials list – or for larger projects with more variables, in the sizing tables. Calculating the total number of squares required will help you to plan out your colourways and guide you on yarn quantities.

Calculating Your Yarn Needs

Each project includes tension information and approximate yarn meterage, so that you will be able to work out yarn requirements. As mentioned in the Yarn section (see page 17), different brands, even of the same yarn weight, all have different meterage per ball. That's why meterage and not ball weight is used to calculate yarn quantities.

The approximate meterage for each project is provided for either the whole project, when worked with an even colour mix, or broken down into 'main colour' and 'contrasting colour' quantities. Once you have chosen which project to work on and decided on your own personal colourway, you can use the number of colours you wish to use to divide the totals given to work out your yarn needs.

For example, if you are making the Summer Squares Top in a size M you will need a meterage of 680 (744yds) for your square colours (see page 155). If you wish to use 6 different colours for your squares then you would need to divide 680 by 6. This means you would need approximately 114 meters (125yds) in each colour for this design.

You can follow the patterns closely, or customise as much as you wish. For each project, the colour balance of the samples shown is listed, so that you can see how a colourway works up in the final piece and use this as guidance if you wish to use the same amounts. Calculating yarn quantities may seem confusing at first, but if you note everything down in your design plan it will be easy to tally up and follow.

If you want to change the length of a piece, for example the Summer Squares Skirt (page 151) or the Groovy Granny Blanket Coat (page 127), use the meterage per square to calculate how much more or less yarn you need. If you want to create a variation on a design or change the yarn weight used for a piece, you will need to recalculate how much yarn is needed.

Please remember that approximate meterage is just that. We all crochet with different tension, and even if our squares are the same size, the meterage can be very slightly different. If, after dividing up your quantities for your chosen yarn, you are very close to using a full ball of yarn, round it up and buy an extra ball. It's always best to err on the side of caution and have a little bit too much yarn rather than run short and lose a game of yarn chicken!

Yarn Calculation Rules

Below are some yarn calculation rules that you can use for DK/Aran weight crochet, which may come in handy if you are customising your makes. Remember when using centimetres in your calculations, you need to divide your total by 100 to get the amount per metre.

Block Treble or Granny Cluster Rows/Rounds
For every row/round of trebles you crochet, on average, you will use 14 times the length of what you are working on in yarn. Use the planned size/length of piece to work out the yarn quantities. For instance, if your row length is 50cm (0.5yd), you would need to allow for approximately 700cm/7m (7yd) of yarn.

Double Crochet Rows/Rounds
For every row/round of double crochet you work, on average, you will use 6 times the length of what you are working on in yarn. For instance, if your row length is 50cm (0.5yd) long you would need to allow for approximately 300cm/3m (3yd) of yarn.

Double Crochet Join
If you are using the double crochet join, you will need approximately 8 times the length of what you are working on in yarn.

If you are calculating yarn for a design with a contrasting colour join, you can use the number of squares to roughly work out the total join using this calculation: (length of 2 sides of single square x total number of squares) x 8.

Open Crochet Join
If you are using the open crochet join you will need approximately 6 times the length of what you are working on in yarn.

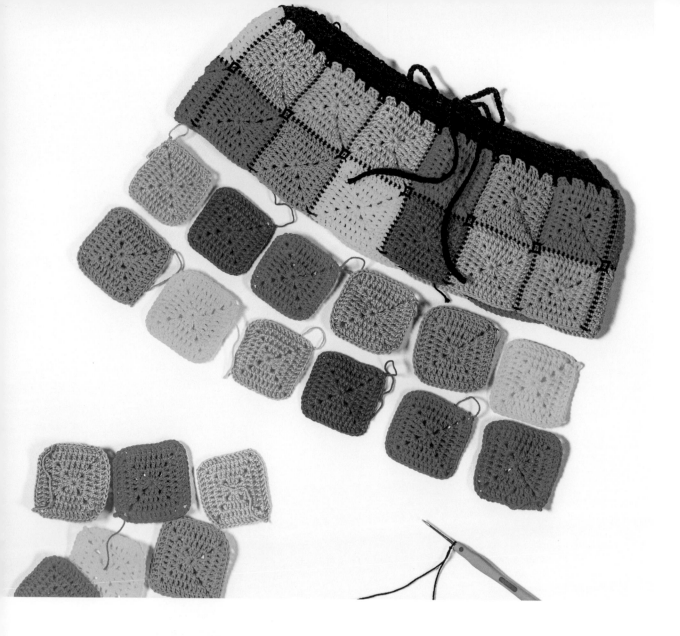

SIZING: FIT AND FEEL

When making garments, understanding their fit and feel is important. The joy of making handmade clothes is about making them fit perfectly. This is where knowing your measurements comes in handy. All the designs in this book are customisable in terms of size, and all the clothing projects are offered in a size range of XS to 5XL.

Measurement Guide

All sizes given in cm and (in).

SIZE	CHEST CIRCUMFERENCE	BODY LENGTH - CENTRE BACK TO WAIST LENGTH	ARMHOLE DEPTH	ARM LENGTH - MEASURED FROM CENTRE BACK TO WRIST
XS	71–76 (28–30)	42 (16½)	16.5 (6½)	68 (26¾)
S	81–86 (32–34)	43 (17)	17.5 (7)	70 (27½)
M	91–97 (35¾–38¼)	43.5 (17⅛)	19 (7½)	72 (28¼)
L	101–107 (39¾–42)	44.5 (17½)	20.5 (8)	74 (29¼)
XL	112–117 (44–46)	45 (17¾)	21.5 (8½)	75 (29½)
2XL	122–127 (48–50)	45.5 (18)	23 (9)	77 (30¼)
3XL	132–137 (52–54)	45.5 (18)	24 (9½)	78 (30¾)
4XL	142–147 (56–58)	47 (18½)	25.5 (10)	80 (31½)
5XL	152–158 (60–62¼)	47 (18½)	26.5 (10½)	81 (32)

As well as your chest measurement, it's good to note down your body length and your centre back to wrist length to get an idea of your sleeve lengths. The table contains the average measurements for the sizes, but we are all shaped differently, and the measurements will be affected by your height and body proportions. Picking how long you like a garment and where you'd like your sleeves to fall is a personal choice and you can customise your garments when planning and making your designs.

Ease

Working out what sort of fit you like for your pieces and understanding ease is important. We are all different, not just in size but in how we like clothes to fit: do you like a fitted piece or a super-oversized feel? Using your favourite clothes to understand what style of fit works best for you is a really useful exercise.

The measurements in the size chart above show actual body measurements; ease is the allowance you add on top of this which indicates the fit of the piece. Each sized design will state the finished piece's size either listed as Flat chest width or Circumference, these pieces already have their ease added, but depending on how you like your fit you may wish to size up or down.

Tight fitting	Body skimming, your actual measurements.
Classic fit	Comfortable fit, slightly larger than actual chest measurement. Approximately 5–10cm (2–4in) larger than your actual measurements.
Loose fit	Slightly oversized fit. Approximately 10–15cm (4–6in) larger than your actual measurements.
Baggy/oversized	Very loose fit. Approximately 15+cm (6+in) larger than your actual measurements.

Project Sizing

The sizing increases in the projects are produced using a number of different methods. Some pieces have more squares added, whereas some designs are altered by adding extension rounds to the original motifs. Some designs may also have extension rounds or rows on joined panels. Each project will state the method that should be used in its instructions.

Because the project designs are made from tessellated squares, they are easy to adapt for the perfect fit. Projects can be enlarged, arm lengths shortened and garments lengthened as desired. These amendments can all be calculated when customising and planning projects.

1

2

3

4

JOINING TECHNIQUES

When it comes to joining your crochet there are many, if not hundreds, of different methods to choose from, all of which have slightly different appearances and uses.

We will be focusing on four different joining methods when constructing the projects in this book: whip stitch, double crochet closed join, crochet open join and join as you go. These are my four favourite joining techniques, and each creates a different effect. A particular join type is suggested for each project, but most can be changed according to personal preference.

For each of the first three joining methods (depending on the project) it is helpful to finish off your chosen block with a long tail fasten off. This means fastening off leaving enough yarn to join along one edge of the block. This works for joins that are in your final row colour and helps reduce the number of ends to sew in at the completion of a make. Each joining method uses a slightly different amounts of yarn so follow the rules below to calculate your tail length. Use these joining techniques, along with each project's instructions and diagrams to help you construct your makes.

1   **WHIP STITCH**
2   **OPEN CROCHET JOIN**
3   **DOUBLE CROCHET JOIN**
4   **JOIN AS YOU GO**

WHIP STITCH

Whip stitch creates a slanted stitch that is flat and appears the same on both the wrong and right side of the piece.

When worked in the colour of one of the squares that is being joined, this method blends in, making a subtle join. This joining method uses the least amount of yarn and can be used easily with all the squares.

STEP BY STEP

1   First, work a long tail fasten off. Fastening off at the last row, measure the long tail by going back and forth along one edge of your square two and a half times.
2   Line up the two squares that you wish to join with right sides facing up.
3   Thread the needle with the long yarn tail, or new yarn if that's what you're using, and pull the needle through the corner stitch of the facing square.
4   Line up the two edges of your squares and stitch through every pair of facing stitches along the edge on the right side of the work. Do not pull too tight to avoid affecting the tension of the square.
5   Sew through the last corner stitch and end the stitching on the wrong side of the work.
6   Fasten off by stitching through the back of the stitches in the same colour and weaving back again. To fully secure, sew in at least 8cm (3¼in) of yarn.

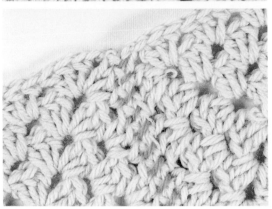

DOUBLE CROCHET JOIN

This is a crochet joining method that creates a firm join and has a neat finish. It is worked on the wrong side of the fabric and creates a slight ridge along the back of the work and a bar-like finish on the right side. This method works well as a design detail and for joining large pieces as it has the same give and stretch as the squares.

The double crochet join uses more yarn than whip stitch but is a quicker and easier way to join, it's also neater if you're using a contrasting colour to join. This technique can be used with all the blocks. You can also trap any loose yarn ends on the edges with this method and reduce the amount of weaving in to do.

STEP BY STEP

1   First, work a long tail fasten off. Fastening off at the last row, measure the long tail by wrapping it around the outer edge of your square two and a half times.
2   Hold the two squares you wish to join, right sides together and wrong sides facing out. If you have one, position the long tail fasten off at the top right corner (left corner if left-handed).
3   Insert the hook through the top right corner chain space of both squares (if left-handed work left to right). If you're using the long tail, hook the yarn through the hole and work a double crochet. If you're using new yarn, start with the yarn on your hook and join with a double crochet.
4   Double crochet through both layers of fabric, working into each pair of stitches along the edges.
5   Double crochet through the corner chain spaces.
6   Fasten off or, if you're continuing to join, chain 1, double crochet into the next set of squares' corner chain space. Repeat steps 4 to 6.

OPEN CROCHET JOIN

The open crochet join works best with the squares that end with their final row in granny clusters. This join mimics the openness of the Granny Squares and creates a fabric with a greater drape that is perfect for clothing.

This crochet joining technique is worked on the wrong side of the work and creates a chain along the back with a bar-like join in the spaces between clusters, which attach the work together.

STEP BY STEP

1   First, work a long tail fasten off. Fastening off at the last row, measure the long tail by wrapping it around the outer edge of your square two and a half times.
2   Hold the two squares you wish to join, right sides together and wrong sides facing out. If you have one, position the long tail fasten off at the top right corner (left corner if left-handed).
3   Insert the hook through the top right corner chain space of both squares (if left-handed work left to right). If you're using the long tail, hook the yarn through the hole and work a double crochet. If you're using new yarn, start with the yarn on your hook and join with a double crochet.
4   Chain 3 stitches, double crochet through the cluster gap of both squares.
5   Repeat step 4 up to the corner chain space.
6   Fasten off or, if you're continuing to join, chain 1, double crochet into the next set of squares' corner chain space. Repeat steps 4 to 6.

JOIN AS YOU GO

Joining as you go works for the motifs in this book if they end with clusters on the final round.

For this join you simultaneously connect your squares and complete the final round of the square. This join doesn't work with all the projects, but it is good for projects where you want an open look. You can use this method to make large areas of fabric, but I prefer to use this technique to join lengths of blocks together in rows and then use the open crochet join to connect the rows together. To use this join, start with one complete square and then work the rest of the row's squares onto it.

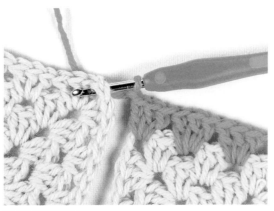

STEP BY STEP

1 Complete your first square of the row (A).
2 Work your next square (B) up until the third round.
3 On your final round of square B complete two sides of the pattern.
4 Hold the two squares back-to-back. At the third corner space, (chain 1, double crochet into corner chain space of square A, chain 1).
5 Continue working clusters along the third edge, but between each cluster double crochet into the equivalent space of square A to join the squares.
6 At the corner chain space, (chain 1, double crochet into corner chain space of square A, chain 1).
7 Work your final edge in the pattern and join.
8 Repeat steps 2 to 7 for all the squares that are to be joined in a row for your project.

A   B

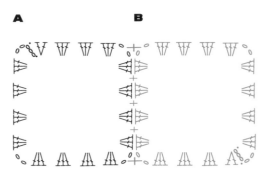

EDGINGS

One of the final stages in the making process, edgings are the cherry on top moment of your project! This final step really finishes off your project giving it its final flourish. The projects in this book use a mix of four different finishes.

PICOT EDGE

Add a bit of fun with this lacey edge. The picot edge is a one-round edging.

STEP BY STEP

1   Double crochet (join with a double crochet if starting the round).
2   Into the next stitch, (double crochet, chain 3, double crochet).
3   Repeat steps 1 to 2 until you reach the beginning of the round.
4   Join with a slip stitch into the first stitch.
5   Fasten off.

DOUBLE CROCHET EDGE

Simple but effective, this is the
easy edging. The double crochet
edge is a minimum one-round
edging, but the number of rounds
can be increased as desired.

STEP BY STEP

1   Work 1 double crochet stitch into each
    stitch (or gap between stitches, depending
    on the pattern).
2   To turn in the corner chain spaces work
    (1 double crochet, chain 1, 1 double crochet)
    into the corner chain space.
3   If you're working over a join of 2 squares:
    double crochet into the corner chain space of
    the first square, double crochet into the join
    stitch, double crochet into the corner chain
    space of the second square.
4   Work double crochet stitch until the end of the
    round and join with a slip stitch into the first
    double crochet to complete the round.
5   If you're repeating more rounds/rows, chain 1
    and repeat double crocheting into each stitch.
6   Fasten off at the desired length.

SPIKE STITCH EDGE

Perfect for creating a firm edge with
a bit of flair. Spike stitch features
a double crochet base and an
elongated double crochet top stitch,
creating a double thickness border.

STEP BY STEP

1 Work double crochet to form the base
   (refer to the project instructions to see how
   many rounds or rows).
2 With a new, contrasting colour on the hook,
   join in with a double crochet into the first stitch
   3 rows down. Pull the yarn through loosely
   to avoid crushing the double crochet base.
3 Double crochet 2 more stitches into the same
   space (the elongated stitch will resemble
   a treble).
4 Miss 2 stitches.
5 Work 3 double crochets into the next stitch
   3 rows below the edge.
6 Repeat steps 4 to 5.
7 Work until the end of the round, join with
   a slip stitch into the first double crochet.
8 Fasten off.

Tip: If you're working over a corner work
(3 double crochet, chain 2, 3 double crochet)
into the same space.

RIB

The classic edging for cuffs and
necklines. The typical knit rib is
replicated in crochet by using a double
crochet stitch and working into the
back loop only. This can feel a little
fiddly at first but it is well worth the
effort to finish off your garments. For
the projects in this book the stitch is
added to the edge and then worked in
rows the opposite way to your work.

STEP BY STEP

Foundation:
A   Join with a double crochet.
B   Chain the number of stitches required
    by the pattern plus 1 turning chain.

Row 1:
A   Miss 1 (turning chain), double crochet
    into each stitch along the foundation chain.
B   Double crochet anchor into the next
    stitch on the project edge (anchor stitch).
C   Double crochet into the next stitch along
    the edge (anchor stitch).

Row 2:
A   Turn, miss 2 (both double crochet
    anchor stitches).
B   Back loop double crochet along the row –
    work stitches through the back strand
    of the stitch top only.

Row 3:
A   Turn, chain 1.
B   Back loop double crochet along the row.
C   Double crochet anchor into the next
    stitch on the project edge (anchor stitch).
D   Double crochet into the next stitch along
    the edge (anchor stitch).
E   Repeat rows 2 and 3 until the end of the round.

Join:
A   On the wrong side, join the ends of the rib with
    double crochet, going through the first and
    last row into each stitch. Fasten off.

SHAPING

Some of the projects in this book require shaping to get the perfect fit or the perfect silhouette. Shaping can be accomplished through a variety of methods: by creating slopes using different stitch lengths; by reducing the number of stitches; by using drawstrings; and by adding additional rows or rounds.

SLOPED SHAPING

The sloped shaping technique is used for shoulder shaping on garment projects (see pages 81 and 87) and for creating the curved join in the Collar project design (see page 113). Adding this subtle shaping to garments gives designs a better fit and a better contour to necklines. These small details will make a big difference to the finished look of your make. The slope is made by using a series of stitches that vary in height: we will use a mix of trebles, half trebles, double crochets and slip stitches. Follow the steps below to calculate your neck slope stitches for each body panel.

STEP BY STEP

1   Mark the desired width of your head hole with stitch markers and remember to allow a bit more space if you're adding a rib finish.
2   Count the stitches from the marked neck edge to the outer edge of the sweater.
3   Divide this number in half. The half closest to the neck opening will be worked in treble stitches.
4   Divide the remaining half by three and split the stitches evenly between slip stitches, double crochets, and half trebles.
5   Working from the outside edge, work in the order of smallest stitch to tallest, working slip stitches first, then double crochet, half trebles and finishing at the treble stitches closest to the neck.
6   Repeat for the opposite shoulder, working from the outside edge towards the neck.

The same principle of sloped stitches is used to shape the Collar project but also includes the use of a double treble stitch. The instructions for this can be found on page 24.

DRAWSTRINGS

Drawstrings can be used to ruche in and constrict your crochet. They involve making a tie and weaving it through your stitches to form a drawstring. They are perfect for making a waist for a garment or for bag openings. This technique is used for the Summer Squares Top and Skirt Set (see page 151) and the Pouch Bag (see page 119).

STEP BY STEP

1   First, make the tie by chaining the number of chain stitches stated on the project page. Then slip stitch through the back bump of the chain stitches all the way along to form a cord.
2   Take your crochet, which should have an open stitch pattern and, starting from the centre point, weave the tie under and over the open stitches back to the starting point. Pull on both ends of the tie to ruche the crochet in to the desired size and tie the cord in a bow to secure.

Decreasing Stitches

The number of stitches in a design can be reduced by working stitches together or by missing stitches. This is a technique that is used in the shaping of some of the projects' sleeves, follow the specific instructions given for each design.

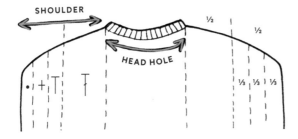

Extension Border Rounds

Some of the patterns in this book call for extension or border rounds as part of their design. These are used for visual effect and for sizing. Border rounds can be worked on individual squares and also around the edges of groups of squares once they have been joined. The rounds are worked as the last round of the square or squares they are edging. To extend individual motifs, follow the extension round instructions for each block pattern. If you are adding border rounds to a group of joined squares, they will be worked in either cluster granny stitch or block stitch rounds, see patterns below.

For example, the Sweater Vest uses extension border rounds to size up individual squares and blocks of squares. The image below shows how this technique can be used to make a size M and a size 3XL.

CLUSTER GRANNY STITCH ROUNDS

Three treble stitches make up one cluster.

Border Round 1:
A   Join in with a slip stitch at any corner chain space.
B   Chain 5 stitches.
C   Work the first cluster into the same space where you joined in. See page 35 for details on the granny cluster.
D   Work 1 cluster into each gap (or between every 3 stitches) up to the corner chain space.
E   Work a cluster into each of the next two joined corner chain spaces.
F   Repeat steps D and E up to the edge's last corner chain space.
G   (Cluster, chain 2, cluster) into the corner chain space.
H   Repeat steps D to G until you have worked the whole way around the block.
I   Treble 2 into the first chain space.
J   Join with a slip stitch into the third chain at the start of the round to complete the round.
K   Fasten off.
L   To add more rounds, follow the Granny Square increase instructions (page 33).

BLOCK STITCH ROUNDS

Border Round 1:
A   Join in with a slip stitch at any corner chain space.
B   Chain 5 stitches.
C   Work 2 trebles into the same space where you joined in.
D   Treble in between each stitch up to the corner chain space.
E   Work 2 trebles into each of the next two joined corner chain spaces.
F   Repeat steps D and E up to the edge's last corner chain space.
G   (Treble 2, chain 2, treble 2) into the corner chain space.
H   Repeat steps D to G until you have worked your whole way around the block.
I   Treble into the first chain space.
J   Join with a slip stitch into the third chain at the start of the round to complete the round.
K   Fasten off.

To add more rounds, follow the Block Square increase instructions (page 37).

Extension Rows

Extension rows are used for sizing and adding length. They are rows that are worked back and forth along an edge, working on the wrong and right side of the work. The number of rows needed, along with what stitch pattern to use, will be described in each project's instructions.

CLUSTER GRANNY STITCH ROWS

Three treble stitches make up one cluster.

Extension Row 1:
A   Join in with a slip stitch at a corner chain space.
B   Chain 3, this replaces the first treble of the row and is your turning chain.
C   Work 2 trebles into the same space where you joined in.
D   Work 1 cluster into each gap up to and including the corner chain space of the edge (if working over joins, work 1 cluster into each chain space).
E   Fasten off or turn if you are extending in the same colour.

Extension Row 2:
A   Continue, or if working in a new colour join in with a slip stitch where you fastened off.
B   Work 1 cluster into each gap along the row.
C   Treble into the third chain of the row below.
D   Fasten off or turn if you are extending in the same colour.

Repeat Rows 1 and 2 as desired.

BLOCK STITCH ROWS

Extension Row 1:
A   Join in with a slip stitch at a corner chain space.
B   Chain 3, this replaces the first treble of the row and is your turning chain.
C   Work 1 treble into the same space where you joined in.
D   Work trebles in the gaps between the stitches up to the corner chain space of the edge (if working over joins work 2 trebles into each chain space).
E   Fasten off or turn if you are extending in same colour.

Extension Row 2:
A   Continue, or if working in a new colour join in with a slip stitch where you fastened off.
B   Chain 3, this replaces the first treble of the row and is your turning chain.
C   Starting in the first gap, Work trebles into each gap between the stitches along edge up to the last stitch. (You are not increasing stitches in the row so stitch count should be the same as round 1).
D   Fasten off or turn if you are extending in the same colour.

Repeat Row 2 as desired.

FINISHING

Now to get that perfect finish! It's time to learn about the final stage of making and how you finish your ends and block your makes.

Dealing with Yarn Ends

Securing yarn ends is a vital part of the making process and ensures that your crochet doesn't unravel; however, it can be a mammoth task – especially if you like using lots of different colours – which is best tackled in small chunks. If you're making up multiple motifs for your projects, sew in your ends as you go to make this an easier process.

You can use a latch hook to secure your yarn ends, or a tapestry needle to weave them into the fabric. When fastening off, leave a tail of at least 8-10cm (3¼–4in) so that you can sew in a minimum of 8cm (3¼in) of yarn. It's also good to remember that when you're working in a block stitch or the final round of a project, if you're edging in double crochet or joining with a solid double crochet join, these ends can be trapped in the stitching to avoid sewing in. Sewing in your ends with a tapestry needle is the most common method. Follow these top tips for good results:

- Sew ends in on the wrong side of the crochet fabric.

- Try to stitch into the same colour yarn to secure discreetly.

- Weave through the stitches in one direction for a short distance and then turn back on yourself, weaving through in the other direction.

- Try to sew through some of the yarn, splitting the stitch/tail to create invisible knots.

- Snip away any excess.

BLOCKING

Blocking out is the term used to describe the process of wetting or steaming a project into place so that it lies flat and keeps its shape. This improves the shape of your crochet piece, which may have become distorted in the making process. Blocking is the final action in the making process and my recommendation is to block a project after it has been joined/finished. Blocking helps even out the tension and flattens out joins as well as straightening stitches and edges; however, remember that not all projects need blocking, and some yarns benefit more from it than others.

The Blocking Process

You can either dampen your work by washing it, by using a water spray or by using a steam iron. I am a lazy blocker, so I always use a steam iron. If you do use a steam iron the most important rule is to always turn your work inside out or onto the wrong side to block. If you are using a particularly delicate yarn such as cashmere, err on the side of caution and opt for the water spray rather than steam. On almost all occasions the steam iron should never touch your fabric! However, some stiff cottons or raffias benefit from being pressed by an iron; for these always use a teatowel in between the iron and piece and test this first on a small sample before trying on a finished piece!

STEP BY STEP

1   The motifs/garments should be pinned out to the correct size on an ironing board or a foam mat using large-headed pins. Particular attention should be paid to any seams or joins to ensure the finished item has straight edges.

2   Once pinned the motifs/garments should be dampened either by spraying with a water or holding a steam iron at least 10cm (4in) above the fabric and spraying it liberally. Make sure the fabric feels damp to the touch. If you are not pinning the work – due to it being a large piece – once damp, it can be flattened and pulled into shape. The steam iron should never touch the crocheted item as the fibres can be irrevocably changed by the heat. Leave the crochet to dry flat before removing the pins.

CROCHET CARE

When you have handmade your own crochet pieces, you want them to last a lifetime! These tips and tricks will help you to care for your crochet.

Storage

Correctly storing your crochet will keep it unstretched and safe from moths. Although you may want to lovingly display any garment you have made in pride of place in your wardrobe, do not hang them up and follow the tips below.

- Crocheted garments should always be stored folded and flat, never hung as they will droop and stretch after a while.

- If your crochet pieces are made from natural fibres, clothes moths can be an issue. If you are storing any pieces for a long time I recommend airtight vacuum bags, these will help keep any nasties away from your natural fibre makes.

- If you ever suspect moths have gotten into any of your woolly or natural fibre pieces, put them in a bag in the freezer for four days to kill the larvae. Inspect the crochet for any holes and darn them where needed.

Washing Crochet

We wash items far too often generally and if only a small area of your crochet is dirty, spot cleaning is recommended; however, sometimes it will be necessary to wash the entire garment. Follow the tips below.

- Always refer to the ball band to find the correct washing instructions for the yarn that has been used. This will avoid any shrinking dilemmas if you're using a natural yarn!

- If in doubt, always wash carefully by hand in cool water, using a detergent suitable for delicate items.

- Do not wring wet items, instead remove any excess water by rolling them in a clean, dry towel.

- If you are using a washing machine, use the most delicate setting or the wool setting and the lowest spin speed. For smaller items it is always a good idea to place them in a laundry bag or pillowcase in the machine.

- Always dry items flat and out of direct sunlight.

Mending

Mending your makes straight away if you see a small hole or loose end will catch any minor damage before it has a chance to become more extensive.

- Loose ends can be woven back into the fabric with a tapestry needle or latch hook. If the loose end is very short and feels too small to thread through a needle normally, start by weaving the needle by itself through the piece, eye-end first to meet the loose end. Then place the yarn tail through the eye to thread the needle and pull through to re-secure your loose end.

- My final top tip is to use a debobbling tool, these work as a razor and take off any pilled yarn bobbles that can form due to friction. This tool will help your creations stay looking freshly made.

THE PROJECTS

SIMPLE SQUARE SWEATER

This simple sweater uses the Granny Square and the Block Square, specially extended to construct a sweater. This is the perfect first garment to make. It sits with a classic, loose fit and its relaxed body and roll-up cuffs make it the ultimate slouchy sweater! Make it in graphic stripes or in colour blocks, whatever you choose; this versatile pattern is easy to adapt. You could easily add extension rounds to the bottom to extend it into a tunic or lengthen it even further to make a dress.

Top Tip

For a summer take on the Simple Square Sweater make it with short sleeves in a bright and light cotton yarn. Halve the number of sleeve squares to make the design a T-shirt shape and don't add the neck rib, instead leave it as an open boat-neck style.

YARN WEIGHT:
Aran (worsted)

HOOK SIZE:
5mm/US size H-8
(or to match tension)

TENSION:
One single square motif =
12 x 12cm (4¾ x 4¾in)

SIZE:
XS–5XL, see chart

EASE:
11–12 cm (4¼–4¾in) loose fit

SAMPLE DESIGNS:
Two design variations:

Main make: Size 2XL.
Worked in alpaca/merino and aran wool. Monochrome body with sleeves worked in the main colour/contrasting colour stripes, using eight contrasting colours. Body worked in extended Granny Squares with sleeves in extended Block Squares.

Variation: Size L.
Worked in cotton aran yarn, six colours. T-Shirt sleeves. Alternating colour body with block contrast colour sleeves. Body worked in extended Granny Squares with sleeves in extended Block Squares.

APPROXIMATE METERAGE:
This will be determined by your chosen design, see chart.

TOTAL SQUARES:
The design uses extended squares: two large squares for the body and eight extended squares for the sleeves.

SIMPLE SQUARE SWEATER
Step by Step Pattern Guide

WORK SHOULDER SHAPING ON BOTH FRONT AND BACK

JOIN SLEEVES X 2

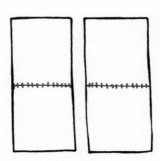
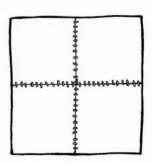

JOIN SWEATER PANELS AND SIDE SEAMS

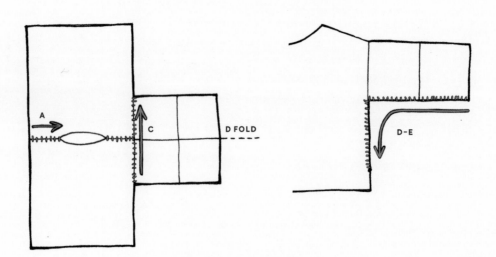

COMPLETE WITH NECK RIB

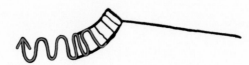

Getting Started

SQUARES

This pattern uses extended square designs; to help with working out yarn quantities the approximate meterage is given in the chart on page 84. You can use these amounts to estimate how much yarn you need in your colour choices.

- Make two large extended Granny Squares for the body following the sizing table.

- Make eight extended Block Squares for the sleeves following the sizing table.

COLOURWAY

Large squares are worked in a two-round, alternating colour stripe pattern. Sleeve squares are worked in a main colour and contrasting colour stripe pattern. The sleeve squares should always end with the main colour: for odd number rounds start in the main colour; for even number rounds start in the contrasting colour.

Instructions

NECK SHAPING

Repeat on each body panel.

A   Mark the desired head hole width on both body panels with stitch markers. It's a good idea to pin the panels together to test the size of the head hole. For reference, on the sample, the flat neck width is 24cm (9½in).

B   Working in the main colour, work the shoulder shaping along the edge. Follow the sloped shaping instructions on page 71 to get your slope right. Work from the outside edge inwards and repeat the slope on each side of the body panel.

JOINING

A   Working in the main colour, join the top edges of the front and back panels together to create the shoulder seam. Place the panels right sides together and join them using the double crochet joining technique (see page 63). Repeat for both shoulders.

B   Join the sleeve squares together into two 2 x 2 panels. First, join the short edges into rows

using the long tail from your long tail fasten off (see page 61), and then join the rows together using the main colour.

C   Now attach the sleeves to the body panels. Placing right sides together, use stitch markers to line up the centre of your sleeve with the shoulder seam. Working on the inside, join the sleeves using the double crochet joining technique. Repeat for both sleeves.

D   Fold the garment at the shoulder seam and join the sleeves and side seams. Using a double crochet join, work from the cuff and along the sleeve. Continue down the side seam of the body panel working in the open crochet join (see page 64). Finish five clusters before the bottom of the panel.

E   Leave five clusters at the bottom open to create a side flap.

F   Fasten off and sew in the ends.

G   Repeat steps D–F to join the second sleeve and side seam.

NECK RIB

In a contrasting colour, work a rib collar that is five double crochets wide.

A   Join in the contrasting colour at the inner neck shoulder seam with a double crochet join.

B   Chain 5 + 1 turning chain.

C   Work the neck rib pattern around edge of the neck hole (see page 69). Work two rows of pattern when working over the side of treble posts.

D   At the last stitch, join the rib by working the first and last rows together with a double crochet join on the inside of garment.

E   Fasten off and sew in the ends.

Top Tips

Extend rounds along the bottom edge
to make the sweater into a tunic or a dress.
If you do extend, join all the way down the
side seams omitting the split.

Extending squares: when you're extending the
pattern and making larger squares, the fabric
can sometimes skew. To keep your squares nice
and straight and square, each time you switch
your yarn colour also change which side of your
work – right side or wrong side – you are joining
into. This means you will be working both into
the wrong and right side of work, creating
no noticeable back or front to the square.

MEASUREMENTS			BODY X 2 SQUARES		SLEEVES X 8 SQUARES	APPROXIMATE METERAGE (YARDAGE)		
SIZE	FLAT CHEST WIDTH IN CM (IN)	BODY LENGTH IN CM (IN)	EXTENDED SQUARES SIZE IN ROUNDS	BODY SIDE EXTENSION ROWS WORK ON EACH OUTSIDE EDGE	EXTENDED SQUARES SIZE IN ROUNDS	TOTAL SQUARES, JOINING, NECK RIB	BODY TOTAL FOR TWO SQUARES	SLEEVES TOTAL FOR EIGHT SQUARES
XS	44 (17¼)	44 (17¼)	16	-	7	940 (1028)	455 (498)	385 (421)
S	49 (19¼)	49 (19¼)	18	-	7	1055 (1154)	570 (623)	385 (421)
M	54 (21¼)	54 (21¼)	20	-	8	1295 (1416)	690 (755)	505 (552)
L	59 (23¼)	59 (23¼)	22	-	8	1450 (1586)	845 (924)	505 (552)
XL	64 (25¼)	64 (25¼)	24	-	8	1600 (1750)	995 (1088)	505 (552)
2XL	69 (27¼)	69 (27¼)	26	-	8	1760 (1925)	1155 (1263)	505 (552)
3XL	74 (29¼)	69 (27¼)	26	+2	9	1965 (2149)	1240 (1356)	625 (684)
4XL	79 (31)	69 (27¼)	26	+4	9	2060 (2253)	1335 (1460)	625 (684)
5XL	84 (33)	69 (27¼)	26	+6	10	2300 (2516)	1440 (1575)	760 (831)

PICK 'N' MIX SWEATER

The balloon-sleeved Pick 'n' Mix Sweater is worked in my favourite, signature shape! It's oversized and relaxed fit make it the perfect everyday sweater. From a spotty graphic mix with stripey sleeves to a classic granny patchwork, mix and match the squares to create endless pattern and colour variations. Grab your hooks and notebooks and start planning the perfect combination for you!

YARN WEIGHT:
DK (light worsted)

HOOK SIZE:
4mm/US size G-6
(or to match tension)

TENSION:
One single square motif =
10 x 10cm (4 x 4in)

SIZE:
XS-5XL, see chart

EASE:
30-40cm (11¾-15¾in)
oversized fit

SAMPLE DESIGNS:
Two design variations both
worked in acrylic DK yarn:

Main make: Size XL.
Graphic pattern worked in five colours. The design combines block colour Granny Squares and Spot Squares. The sleeves are worked in colour bands, the body is worked in a main colour with the addition of randomly placed Spot Squares with their last rounds worked in the main colour for the body.

Variation: Size XL.
Granny Squares with the final round worked in black. Worked in a random colour mix using 12 colours and a black base. Sleeves are left three-quarter length without a cuff.

APPROXIMATE METERAGE:
16m (17½yd) per square, with a long tail fasten off. Total meterage will be determined by your chosen size.

TOTAL SQUARES:
90-144, total will be determined by your chosen size, see chart.

PICK 'N' MIX SWEATER
Step by Step Pattern Guide

WORK BODY PANELS X 2

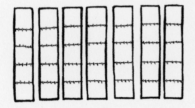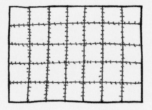

**ADD BODY SIZING ROWS (1)
AND ADD SHOULDER SHAPING (2)**

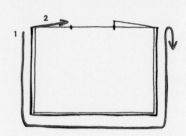

WORK SWEATER JOINING

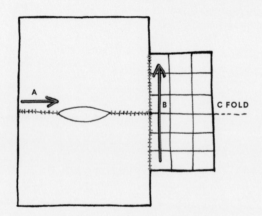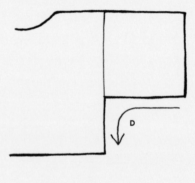

ADD CUFFS (1) AND BOTTOM EDGING (2)

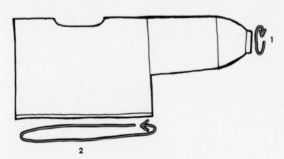

COMPLETE WITH NECK RIB

Getting Started

SQUARES

Follow the chart on page 91 to make the correct number of squares for your sweater. The sample design uses the Granny and Spot Squares, so use the open crochet join for construction – any motifs with a granny-cluster edge can be used.

If you are following the sample design, plan out your make to determine how many Spot Squares you want to mix into the front and back panels. Fasten off the squares with a long tail (see page 61) for the open crochet joining method.

COLOURWAY

The design is worked with contrasting sleeves and body. The body is worked in a main block colour with the addition of colour spots – Spot Squares worked with contrasting centres and main colour final rounds. Granny Squares are worked in a single colour. Sleeves are worked in four contrasting colours. For XS–S divide the number of sleeves squares by four colours and work the cuff in the final stripe colour. For sizes M–5XL divide the sleeve squares by three colours and work the cuffs in the fourth contrast colour.

Instructions

BODY PANELS

A   Lay out the body squares in two panels to make sure the colours and square patterns are distributed evenly.

B   Working in the main colour, join the squares together into two panels using the open crochet joining technique (see page 64). First, join the short edges into rows and then join the longer rows together.

BODY SIZING ROWS

Refer to the chart to see if you need to add body sizing rows along the edges of the front and back panels. If you do, work on the outside edge in a U-shape (not working the top edge).

A   Join in at the top outside edge corner chain space and, using the main colour, work the additional rows in granny stitch extension rows.

B   Follow the granny stitch extension rows pattern on page 73. In the bottom corner chain spaces work, (cluster, chain 2, cluster).

C   Repeat rows to size, see chart for reference.

D   Fasten off.

E   Repeat on the second panel.

SHOULDER SHAPING

Repeat for each body panel.

A   Mark desired head hole width on both panels with stitch markers. It's best to pin the panels together to test the size of the head hole. For reference, the sample flat neck width is 22cm (8¾in).

B   Using the main colour, work the shoulder shaping, following the stitch rule to get the right slope (see page 71). Work from the outside edge inwards and repeat the slope on each side of body panel. If you are working over extension rows, work two stitches over each treble post.

SLEEVES

Join the squares together into two panels using the open crochet joining technique.

A   Lay the sleeve panels out to arrange the colour spread/design.

B   Join the short edges into rows using the yarn from the long tail fasten off.

C   Join the longer rows together in new yarn. If you are working striped sleeves, use a colour to match one of the stripe rows you are joining to get an invisible join.

SWEATER JOINING

A   Working in the main colour, join the top edge of the front and back panels together to create the shoulder seam. Place right sides together and, working on the inside, join using the double crochet joining technique (see page 63). Repeat on both shoulders.

B   Attach the sleeves to the body panels. Place right sides together and use stitch markers to help you line up the centre of the sleeve with the shoulder seam. Working on the inside, join using the open crochet joining technique (see page 64). Repeat for the other sleeve.

- Makes with extension rows on the top of shoulder will have two joined clusters.
- On sleeves where the joins line up to the shoulder seam, join in at sleeve corner

chain spaces and on either side of
the shoulder join between trebles.

- For sleeves where the centre of a square
  lines up with the shoulder seam, join at
  a sleeve square gap and at the shoulder
  seam join stitch.

C   To join sleeves and side seams, fold the
garment in half along the shoulder seam
with right sides facing.

D   Using the main colour and the open crochet
joining technique, work from the cuff to the
sweater's bottom edge, in an L-shape. Work
along the arm edge from the cuff till you reach
the body (if you have made the sleeve in colour
stripes, use long tails to join each section) and
continue, working down to the bottom edge
of the sweater.

E   Fasten off.

F   Repeat steps D and E for the other side.

G   Sew in all joining yarn ends.

CUFFS

Use the cuff contrasting colour and repeat for
both sleeves. If your design size doesn't call for
extension rounds (see chart) skip forward to
Cuff Decrease Round 1.

Cuff Extension Round 1

A   Working in a contrasting colour, join in with
a slip stitch at a corner chain space at the
under-cuff point.

B   Chain 3 (counts as 1 treble).

C   Treble 2 into the first gap.

D   Granny cluster into each gap and into each
chain space over joins of round.

E   Join with a slip stitch into the third chain
at beginning to complete round.

Cuff Extension Rounds 2-5

A   Chain 3 (counts as 1 treble).

B   Treble 2 into the first gap.

C   Granny cluster into each gap and into
each chain space over joins of round.

D   Join with a slip stitch into the third chain
at beginning to complete round.

E   Repeat for the number of cuff extension
rounds given for your chosen size (see chart).

Cuff Decrease Round 1

A   Chain 3 (counts as 1 treble).

B   Treble into the first gap.

C   Treble 2 into each gap of the round.

D   Join with a slip stitch into the third chain
at beginning to complete round.

Cuff Decrease Round 2

A   Chain 2, treble into same gap.

B   Treble 2 together into each gap of round.
(For sizes XS/S work a stitch repeat of:
treble 2 together in gap, treble 2 in gap)
in each gap of round.)

C   Join with a slip stitch into the top of the
first treble to complete round.

Cuff Rib

A   Chain 6 + 1 turning chain.

B   Work the rib edging pattern around edge
(see page 69).

C   At the last stitch, join the rib by working the
first and last rows together with a double
crochet join on the inside of the garment.

D   Fasten off and sew in yarn ends.

BOTTOM EDGING

A   Join in with the main colour at the side seam
and work one round of cluster granny stitch
extension rows, omitting step E (see page 73).

B   Join with a slip stitch into the third chain
at beginning to complete round.

C   Fasten off and sew in yarn ends.

NECK RIB

Work a six-double-crochet wide rib in the
main colour.

A   Using the main colour, join in at the inner neck
shoulder seam with a double crochet join.

B   Chain 6 + 1 turning chain.

C   Work rib pattern around the neck edge
(see page 69). When working over the side
of treble posts around the neck, work two
rows of rib pattern over them.

D   At the last stitch, join the rib by working the
first and last rows together with a double
crochet join on the inside of garment.

E   Fasten off and sew in yarn ends.

FINISHING

Block if desired, following the instructions
on page 74.

Top Tip

For a boxier look, you can adapt the sleeves to produce a sweater with a very different feel. For this variation, three cuff extension rounds are worked, and the sleeves are fastened off to give a wide three-quarter length sleeve. If you are making a size XS/S reduce the sleeve length by one square.

MEASUREMENTS			BODY X 2		SLEEVES X 2		TOTAL SQUARES			APPROXIMATE METERAGE (YARDAGE)		
SIZE	FLAT CHEST WIDTH IN CM (IN)	BODY LENGTH IN CM (IN)	SQUARES WIDTH X DEPTH	SIZING ROWS	SQUARES DEPTH X LENGTH	CUFF EXTENSION ROUNDS	BODY	SLEEVES	ALL	TOTAL	BODY SQUARE SIZING ROWS JOINING NECK	SLEEVES SQUARES JOINING CUFFS
XS	50 (19¾)	52 (20½)	5 x 5	–	5 x 4	–	50	40	90	1635 (1788)	935 (1023)	700 (766)
S	56 (22)	55 (21¾)	5 x 5	+3	5 x 4	–	50	40	90	1720 (1881)	1020 (1115)	700 (766)
M	62 (24½)	53 (21)	6 x 5	+1	6 x 3	+5	60	36	96	1825 (1996)	1110 (1214)	715 (782)
L	70 (27½)	52 (20½)	7 x 5	–	6 x 3	+5	70	36	106	1945 (2127)	1230 (1345)	715 (782)
XL	76 (30)	55 (21¾)	7 x 5	+3	6 x 3	+2	70	36	106	2055 (2247)	1390 (1520)	665 (727)
2XL	82 (32¼)	63 (24¾)	8 x 6	+1	6 x 3	+2	96	36	132	2330 (2548)	1665 (1821)	665 (727)
3XL	86 (34)	65 (25½)	8 x 6	+3	6 x 3	+2	96	36	132	2440 (2668)	1790 (1958)	650 (711)
4XL	90 (35½)	62 (24½)	9 x 6	–	6 x 3	+1	108	36	144	2515 (2750)	1865 (2040)	650 (711)
5XL	96 (37¾)	65 (25½)	9 x 6	+3	6 x 3	–	108	36	144	2700 (2953)	2070 (2264)	630 (689)

BUCKET HAT

A fun, frilly bucket hat with a short brim that will be a great addition to your favourite summer or winter outfits alike! This speedy make can be made in cool cottons or woolly winter yarns to complement your outfits all year round. The hat's simple shape is made up of five squares. Why not make one to match every outfit?

YARN WEIGHT:
Aran (worsted)

HOOK SIZE:
5mm/US size H-8
(or to match tension)

TENSION:
One single square motif =
12.5 x 12.5cm (5 x 5in)

SIZE:
One size, approximately
56cm (22in) around the head.
To make a slightly smaller
or larger hat, size down
or up a hook size.

SAMPLE DESIGNS:
Two design variations:

Variation 1: Granny Square;
worked in 2 alternating
colours, baby alpaca/
merino yarn

Variation 2: Spot Square;
worked in a random mix of
8 colours, aran wool yarn

APPROXIMATE METERAGE:
Total = 160m (175yd)

Main colour = 120m (132yd)

Contrasting colours =
40m (44yd)

TOTAL SQUARES:
Five.

Top Tips

You can use different colours for each round and the brim as well as mixing motifs to give a patchwork festival vibe!

Size down your yarn and hook for a kids' size hat.

BUCKET HAT
Step by Step Pattern Guide

CROWN TOP JOIN

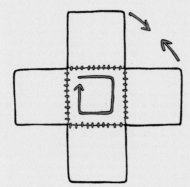

CROWN SIDES JOIN

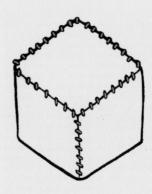

CROWN ROUND 1 EXTENSION

BRIM ROUNDS

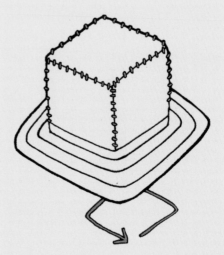

Getting Started

SQUARES
Make five squares. Finish four of the squares with the double crochet join long tail fasten off (see page 61). The sample variations are made in Granny and Spot Squares but any motif and any motif combination can be used.

COLOURWAY
For 2 colour variations, make sure your final round is in the main colour.
- Round 1: Contrast colour.
- Round 2: Main colour.
- Round 3: Contrast colour.
- Round 4: Main colour.

Instructions

JOINING
Using the main colour only, make up the hat and create the brim.

Crown join
A   Create a net of your hat with the squares. Working on the wrong side and using the double crochet join (see page 63), join the four long-tail squares to the fifth central square (top of hat). (14 double crochet to make each edge join.)
B   Fold down the side edges on the wrong side of work to form a box shape – which makes up the crown of the hat – and join using the double crochet join.

Crown Round 1
Working along the open edge.
A   Turn the crown the right way out with the join seams on the inside.
B   Join in with a slip stitch at any corner chain space.
C   Chain 3, treble 2 into the same corner chain space.
D   If the final round of your squares is treble clusters, crochet 3 trebles (1 cluster) into the next and each subsequent gap, including the corner chain spaces at the joins (20 clusters in all).
E   Join with a slip stitch into the third chain at the start of the round to complete the extension round of the crown.

Brim Round 1
A   Chain 3, treble into the same stitch.
B   Working into the top of the stitch, 2 trebles into every stitch from Crown Round 1. This is the increase round and what shapes the brim (total of 120 stitches).
C   Join with a slip stitch into the third chain at the start of the round to complete the first round of the brim.

Brim Round 2
A   Chain 3.
B   Treble into the top of each stitch from the previous round.
C   Join with a slip stitch into the third chain at the start of the round.

Brim Round 3
A   Repeat Brim Round 2.
B   Fasten off and sew in yarn ends.

Top Tip
If you've used the Block or Ferris Wheel Squares, the final round will be single trebles not 3 treble clusters. So for Crown Round 1 work step C, then for step D skip 3 trebles and work a 3 treble cluster into the gap between the next 2 trebles. Repeat this to the next corner chain space, and work the last 3 treble cluster into the corner chain space. Repeat steps C and D to the end (total of 20 clusters).

QUILT CARDIGAN

Say hello to the Quilt Cardy, a showstopper piece for your woolly wardrobe! This chunky-weight number, inspired by patchwork quilts, is here to wrap you up in cosy goodness. This design is worked in groups of squares edged with border rounds to give it its distinctive pattern.

YARN WEIGHT:
Chunky (Bulky) or two strands of DK (light worsted) held together can be used

HOOK SIZE:
7mm/US size K-10½–L-11 (or to match tension)

TENSION:
One single square motif = 16 x 16cm (6¼ x 6¼in)

SIZE:
XS–5XL, see chart

EASE:
12cm (4¾in) ease, loose fit

SAMPLE DESIGNS:
Two design variations:

Main make: Worked in merino/ alpaca chunky yarn using the Ferris Wheel design. Main colour white with seven contrasting colours worked in a random mix. Small three-round Block Squares used for the sleeves.

Variation: Worked in two strands of acrylic DK held together using the Block Square design. Sleeveless waistcoat design. Main colour black with seven contrasting colours worked in a random mix.

APPROXIMATE METERAGE:
Total meterage is dependent on size made, see chart.

TOTAL SQUARES:
Body = 15 full motifs with added rounds for sizing, see chart.

Sleeves = total will vary depending on size, see chart.

QUILT CARDIGAN
Step by Step Pattern Guide

JOIN FRONT AND BACK PANELS

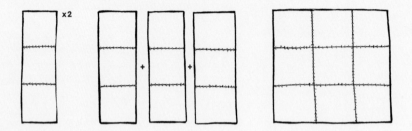

ADD EXTENSION ROWS ON SIDE EDGES IF NEEDED FOR SIZE

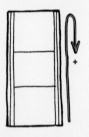

ADD BORDER ROUNDS TO FRONTS AND BACK

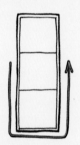

JOIN SLEEVE PANELS AND ADD EXTENSION ROWS IF NEEDED

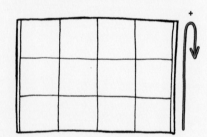

JOIN CARDY PANELS AND SLEEVES

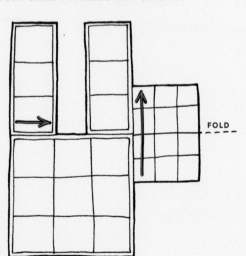

FOLD

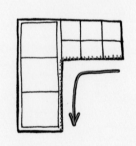

JOIN CARDY PANELS AND SLEEVES

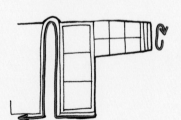

ADD LAPEL ROUNDS AND CUFF EDGING

Getting Started

SQUARES

This design uses a mix of full-size motifs and smaller squares. Full-size squares are used for the body panels: the sample uses the Ferris Wheel motif, but any square can be used. For sizes XL–2XL make your main squares one round larger. For sizes 3XL–5XL make your main squares two rounds larger. Make 15 full-size squares.

One single square motif (XS–M) = 16 x 16cm (6¼ x 6¼in)

One single square motif + 1 (XL–2XL) = 19 x 19cm (7½ x 7½in)

One single square motif + 2 (3XL–5XL) = 22 x 22cm (8¾ x 8¾in)

Smaller squares are used for the sleeves. The number of squares required varies depending on the size, see chart on page 101 for the number needed. Smaller squares are worked for three rounds in the Block Square design. Finish off your squares and sew in yarn ends.

Smaller three-round square (for sleeves) = 12 x 12cm (4¾ x 4¾in)

COLOURWAY

This piece is worked with a main colour and mixed contrasting colours. The main colour is used for joining and for alternate rounds of the border and sizing rows. To calculate contrasting colour quantities, use the approximate meterage chart (on page 100). Divide the total approximate meterage for your squares contrast colour by the number of colours you wish to use. Select one of your contrasting colours for the extension rows/rounds and another for the lapel. Add their total meterage to your calculated amount per colour. Full-size squares: work these in a mix of your contrasting colours, changing each round. Sleeve squares: change colour each round:

- Round 1: contrast colour
- Round 2: main colour
- Round 3: contrast colour

Instructions

BODY PANELS

Using your main colour, join the body squares together to make the body panel. Join the squares using the double crochet joining technique (see page 63).

A   Lay out the squares for your two front panels of three squares and your back panel of nine squares. Laying out your panels will help you to distribute the different colours evenly.

B   Join the front panels into two strips of three.

C   Repeat the process for the back panel first joining into three strips of three, and then join along the long edges to produce the whole block.

SIZING ROWS (2XL-5XL)

Refer to the chart to see if you need to add body sizing rows along all the outer edges of your body panels. Working on the side edges of the panels and following the block stitch extension rows pattern (see page 73), add additional rows to the appropriate size. Work your first rows in the main colour and then alternate between your chosen rows/rounds contrasting colour and your main colour for any subsequent rows.

BORDER ROUNDS

Border rounds are added to each of your body panels. Use the block stitch extension rounds pattern (see page 72) for the number of rounds needed. Alternate between the main colour and the rows/rounds contrast colour. Start your first round in the main colour or continue the colour pattern if your size already has sizing rows added. If working oversizing extension rows on, to continue the stitch pattern work 2 trebles over the side of the treble posts.

SLEEVE PANELS

Using the main colour, join the sleeve squares together using the double crochet joining technique (see page 63).

A   Lay out the squares for the two sleeves. Laying out your panels will help you to distribute the different colours evenly.

B   First, join the short edges into rows, and then join the longer rows together.

C   Sew in yarn ends.

SLEEVE SIZING:

Refer to the chart to see if you need to add sleeve sizing rows along the outer edges of the panels (under arm).

Working on the three-square-long side edges,

add additional rows to size using the block stitch extension rows pattern. Work your first rows in the main colour and then alternate between your chosen rows/rounds contrasting colour and your main colour for any subsequent rows.

JOINING THE SLEEVES TO THE BODY

A If the body panels ended in a contrast colour, work in the main colour and if the body panels ended in the main colour, work in a contrast colour. Join the top edge of the front panels to the back panel to create the shoulder seam. Place right sides together and work on the inside using the double crochet joining technique. Work from the outer edge inwards when joining to help line up your panels.

B Attach the sleeves to the joined body. Use stitch markers to line up the centre of your sleeve with the shoulder seam. Place right sides together and, working on the inside, join with the main colour using the double crochet joining technique.

C Join the sleeves and side seams. Fold the garment in half along the shoulder seam, with right sides facing. Using the double crochet joining technique, work from the cuff to the bottom edge of the cardigan in an L shape.

D Start from the edge the cuff and work along the arm to the body. If the sleeve panels ended in a contrast colour, work in the main colour and if the sleeve panels ended in the main colour, work in a contrast colour.

E Continue to join, working down to the bottom edge of the cardy. Follow the colour rules in step D. Change colour for lower join if necessary.

F Fasten off.

G Repeat steps D–F for the other side.

H Sew in all joining yarn ends.

CUFF ROUNDS

Refer to the chart for the number of rounds to add for each size and repeat for each cuff. Work the first round in the main colour and then alternate with contrasting colours.

Round 1

A Join into a corner chain space with a slip stitch at the under-cuff point.

B Chain 3 (counts as 1 treble).

C Treble between each stitch and chain space of round.

D Repeat steps A–D for any extra rounds following colour order. Join in between any stitches under the cuff to start the next round.

Cuff trim

A Working in the lapel contrast colour, join in at any stitch under the cuff.

B Chain 1.

C Using the double crochet edge technique (see page 67), work 3 rounds.

D Fasten off and sew in ends.

LAPEL

Round 1

A Working in the lapel contrast colour, join in with a slip stitch at the centre back.

B Chain 3 (counts as 1 treble).

C Treble between each stitch along the round.

D (Treble 2, chain 2, treble 2) into corner chain space.

E Repeat steps C and D until the end of the round.

F Join with a slip stitch into the third chain from the beginning.

G Fasten off or repeat the round. See chart for the number of lapel rounds to add for each size.

FINISHING

Block if desired, following the instructions on page 74. If your lapel corners aren't lying flat this will straighten them out.

SIZE	TOTAL METERAGE (YARDAGE)	MAIN COLOUR METRE (YARD)	CONTRAST COLOUR METRE (YARD)		
			SQUARES	ROWS/ROUNDS	LAPEL
XS	1050 (1148)	295 (323)	540 (591)	40 (44)	175 (192)
S	1130 (1236)	320 (350)	540 (591)	125 (137)	145 (159)
M	1210 (1324)	405 (443)	600 (656)	100 (110)	105 (115)
L	1355 (1482)	365 (399)	755 (826)	35 (39)	200 (219)
XL	1440 (1575)	365 (399)	755 (826)	155 (170)	165 (181)
2XL	1585 (1733)	565 (618)	755 (826)	140 (153)	125 (137)
3XL	1665 (1821)	340 (372)	960 (1050)	185 (203)	180 (197)
4XL	1825 (1996)	390 (427)	960 (1050)	285 (312)	190 (208)
5XL	1945 (2127)	455 (498)	960 (1050)	335 (367)	195 (214)

Top Tips

Ditch the sleeves and make this design into a waistcoat. Add a couple of edging rounds along the sleeve head to finish. For more colour, mix up your border rounds by using more than one contrasting colour.

You could use a lux chunky wool for a very special treat, but this piece would also whip up perfectly if you plied two strands of acrylic DK together for a more budget-friendly project! If you are working with two strands of DK remember to double the meterage required.

MEASUREMENTS			BODY FRONT SQUARES 1 X 3 (X2) BACK SQUARES 3 X 3				SLEEVES SMALLER THREE-ROUND SQUARES SLEEVE PANELS X 2				EDGING
SIZE	FLAT CHEST WIDTH IN CM (IN)	BODY LENGTH IN CM (IN)	SQUARE EXTENSION ROUNDS	TOTAL SQUARES	EDGE ROWS	BORDER EDGE SIZING ROUNDS	SQUARES PER SLEEVE (D X L)	TOTAL SQUARES	EDGE SIZING ROWS	CUFF EXTENSION ROUNDS	LAPEL ROUNDS
XS	51 (20)	57 (22½)	-	15	-	1	3 x 3	18	+2	3	4
S	54 (21¼)	58.5 (23)	-	15	-	2	3 x 3	18	+3	3	3
M	57 (22½)	60 (23¾)	-	15	-	3	4 x 3	24	-	3	2
L	60 (23¾)	66 (26)	+1	15	-	1	4 x 3	24	-	4	4
XL	63 (24¾)	67.5 (26½)	+1	15	-	2	4 x 3	24	-	4	3
2XL	69 (27¼)	69 (27¼)	+1	15	+1	3	4 x 3	24	+1	3	2
3XL	72 (28¼)	73.5 (29)	+2	15	+1	1	4 x 3	24	+1	3	3
4XL	78 (30¾)	73.5 (29)	+2	15	+3	1	4 x 3	24	+2	2	3
5XL	84 (33)	73.5 (29)	+2	15	+5	1	4 x 3	24	+2	1	3

LAZY DAISY TOP

The Lazy Daisy Top is the perfect beach cover-up. Its oversized shape, lacy fabric and open joins mean it's a light garment with great drape. There is a deep V-neck at the front and back, with handy neck ties to stop it falling off your shoulders, and it's edged in a delicate picot trim to round off that lacy feeling. It doesn't have to be just for summer, pair it with a roll neck for a top that works in all seasons. This piece uses a lot of squares, so it's perfect to make in small batches on lazy afternoons.

YARN WEIGHT:
DK (light worsted)

HOOK SIZE:
4mm/US size G-6
(or to match tension)

TENSION:
One single square motif =
10 x 10cm (4 x 4in)

SIZE:
XS–5XL, see chart for measurements

EASE:
35–80cm (13¾–31½in), oversized

SAMPLE DESIGN:
The sample was made in cotton DK in size 3XL–5XL. The Flower Square was used with a main colour final round and contrasting colours in the centre. Main colour white with six contrasting colours worked in a random pattern mix.

APPROXIMATE METERAGE:
13.3m (14½yd) per square, including long tail fasten off.

Main colour = 7.2m (8yd)

Contrasting colours = 6.1m (6¾yd)

Total meterage is dependent on the size made, see chart.

TOTAL SQUARES:
72–192, dependent on the size made, see chart.

MEASUREMENTS			BODY X 2	TOTAL	APPROXIMATE METERAGE (YARDAGE)		
SIZE	FLAT CHEST WIDTH IN CM (IN)	BODY LENGTH IN CM (IN)	SQUARES WIDTH X DEPTH	SQUARES 2 BODY PANELS	TOTAL	MAIN COLOUR JOINING TRIM & OUTER ROUNDS	CONTRAST COLOURS SQUARE INNER ROUNDS
XS–S	60 (23¾)	60 (23¾)	6 x 6	72	1215 (1329)	675 (738)	540 (591)
M–L	80 (31½)	60 (23¾)	8 x 6	96	1515 (1657)	795 (870)	720 (787)
XL–2XL	100 (39½)	70 (27½)	10 x 7	140	2065 (2258)	1015 (1110)	1050 (1148)
3XL–5XL	120 (47¼)	80 (31½)	12 x 8	192	2815 (3079)	1375 (1504)	1440 (1575)

LAZY DAISY TOP
Step by Step Pattern Guide

JOIN SQUARES IN FOUR PANELS

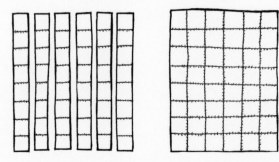

x4

JOIN SHOULDER SEAM IN PANEL PAIRS (1)
AND JOIN CENTRE FRONT TO MAKE NECKLINE (2)

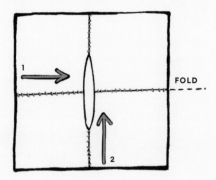

FOLD

MARK AND JOIN BOTH SIDE SEAMS (1).
ADD ARM HOLE (2) AND BOTTOM EDGING (3)

COMPLETE WITH
NECK EDGING

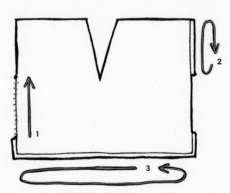

Getting Started

SQUARES
Follow the chart to make the correct number of squares for your Lazy Daisy Top. Fasten the squares off with a long tail (see page 61) for the open crochet joining method. The sample features the Flower Square; however, any motif with a granny cluster edge can be used with the open join.

COLOURWAY
The main colour is used for the final rounds of the squares, for joining and for edging. A mix of colours is used for the inner rounds. Change colour each round for the inners, using a mix of six colours, evenly spread in a random mix.

Instructions

BODY
Working in the main colour.
A   Lay out the squares for the front and back following the measurements in the chart.
B   Join the squares together into vertical strips using the open crochet joining method (see page 64).
C   Separate the strips to form a left and right side for the front, and a left and right side for the back so that you have four panels.
D   Working on the wrong side of the squares, join the strips to complete each panel. Join along the long edges in the open crochet join. You should now have four joined panels.
E   Join a pair of front and back panels by working the open crochet join along the top edge of the shoulder seam, crocheting on the inside of the garment.
F   Repeat this process to join the remaining panel pair.
G   Sew in all joining ends.

NECKLINE/CENTRE FRONT
A   Lay the panels out and decide on the depth of the neckline by measuring along the centre seam from the shoulders down.
B   Mark the depth on both on the front and back of the garment using a stitch marker. This point will be the same on both sides.
C   Working from the bottom front edge up,

join the panels along the centre seam using the open crochet join.
D   Repeat the joining process on the back panel.
E   Sew in all joining ends.

SIDE JOIN
Work on the inside of the garment and repeat for both sides.
A   Mark the armhole depth using a stitch marker. For sizes XS–L, mark at 2.5 squares down from shoulder. For sizes XL–5XL, mark at 3 squares down from shoulder.
B   Mark the side flap using a stitch marker. For sizes XS–L, mark at 1 square up from bottom edge. For sizes XL–2XL mark at 2 squares up from bottom edge. For sizes 3XL–5XL, mark at 3 squares up from bottom edge.
C   Join the side seams together between the two marked points using the open crochet join.
D   Sew in all joining ends.

ARMHOLE EDGING
Work on the inside of the garment and repeat for both sides.

Round 1
A   Join in with a slip stitch at the underarm cluster gap.
B   Chain 3 (counts as 1 treble).
C   Work 2 trebles into the same gap.
D   Treble 3 into each cluster gap and chain space of the round.
E   Join with a slip stitch into the third chain to complete the round.

Round 2
A   Chain 3 (counts as 1 treble).
B   Treble 3 into each cluster gap up to the end of the round.
C   Treble 2 into the first space to complete the cluster.
D   Join with a slip stitch into the third chain to complete the round.

Round 3
A   Chain 1.
B   Double crochet into each stitch of round.
C   Join with a slip stitch into the first chain to complete the round.

Round 4
A   Chain 1.

B   Using the picot edge stitch pattern
    (see page 66) complete the round.
C   Join with a slip stitch into the first chain
    to complete the round.
D   Fasten off and sew in yarn ends.

BOTTOM EDGING

A   Join in at the side seam join with a slip stitch.
B   Chain 1.
C   Double crochet into each stitch along the edge
    up to the bottom edge corner chain space.
D   (1 double crochet, 1 chain, 1 double crochet)
    into corner.
E   Repeat steps C and D.
F   Double crochet into each stitch along the edge
    until you reach the start of the side seam.
G   Working into the next panel repeat steps C–F.
H   Join with a slip stitch into the first chain to
    complete the round.
I   Fasten off and sew in yarn ends.

NECK EDGING

Working on the right side of the garment.

Round 1

A   Join in at the corner chain space on the
    inner shoulder seam with a slip stitch.
B   Chain 3 (counts as 1 treble).
C   Work 2 trebles into the same gap.
D   Treble 3 into each cluster gap and chain
    space along the edge up to the gap before
    the centre join.
E   Double treble 2 together, working a part of the
    stitch in each space either side of the centre
    join. This decreases the stitches and shapes
    the neck.
F   Treble 3 into each cluster gap and chain space
    along the edge up to the gap before the next
    centre join.
G   Repeat step E.
H   Treble 3 into each cluster gap and chain space
    along the edge until you reach the last space.
I   Join with a slip stitch into the third chain to
    complete the round.

Round 2

A   Chain 1.
B   Double crochet into each stitch up to the two
    stitches before the 'double treble 2 together'
    in the round below.
C   In the next stitch, work the first part of a
    double crochet 2 together, miss the two

stitches over the centre join decrease,
and complete your double crochet 2
together in the next stitch.
D   Repeat steps B and C.
E   Double crochet along the edge up
    to the first stitch.
F   Join with a slip stitch into the first chain
    to complete the round.

Round 3

A   On the back of garment, use stitch markers
    to mark one square down from the top on
    both sides.
B   Chain 1.
C   Using the picot edge stitch (see page 66)
    work up to the stitch marker.
D   Chain 50 stitches.
E   Working into the back bump of the chain,
    slip stitch back along chain to create a tie.
F   Double crochet anchor into the next
    neck stitch.
G   Repeat steps C–F.
H   Using the picot edge stitch, work until the
    end of the round.
I   Join with a slip stitch into the first chain
    to complete the round.
J   Fasten off and sew in yarn ends.

Finishing

Block if desired, following the instructions
on page 74.

Top Tips

This make is perfect for using the
join-as-you-go method (see page 65).
Make all your squares up until the final
round and use the join-as-you-go
method to work the final round in the
main colour and construct your strips.
Once you have made the strips you can
join these with the open join method
along the long edges.

SPOTS AND STRIPES BLANKET

This blanket works perfectly as a throw for the couch, at the end of a bed or as a picnic blanket. The join-as-you-go construction makes this project come together quickly and it packs a colourful punch with only half the ends to sew in!

YARN WEIGHT:
Chunky (bulky)

HOOK SIZE:
6mm/US size J-10
(or to match tension)

TENSION:
One single square motif =
14 x 14cm (5½ x 5½in)

SIZE:
One size, 110 x 150cm
(43¼ x 59in)

SAMPLE DESIGN:
Acrylic yarn, the squares are worked in seven contrasting colours with white as the main colour.

APPROXIMATE METERAGE:
Total meterage = 1,770m
(1,936yd)

Main colour = 680m (744yds)

Contrast colours =
1090m (1192yds)

TOTAL SQUARES:
42

Top Tips

Extend this design by adding more squares to your strips to widen the blanket, or more repeats of your strips to lengthen it.

This design is easy to scale down; use aran or DK yarn to make a smaller blanket.

SPOTS AND STRIPES BLANKET
Step by Step Pattern Guide

JOIN THE SQUARES AS YOU GO INTO
STRIPS. ADD ROWS TO EDGE OF STRIPS

ADD ROW OF MAIN COLOUR
TO ALL STRIP INSIDE EDGES

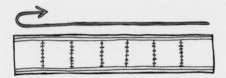
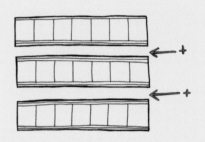

JOIN STRIPS IN PAIRS IN THE JOIN AS YOU GO METHOD AND JOIN STRAPS

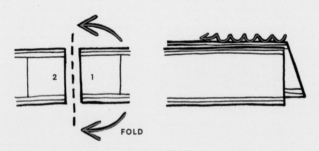

ADD LONG EDGE EXTENSION
ROWS IN CONTRASTING COLOUR

ADD FINAL BORDER ROUND
IN MAIN COLOUR

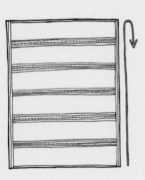
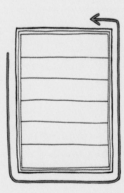

Getting Started

SQUARES
The sample design uses the Spot Square; however, you can use the join-as-you-go construction method for any motif with a granny cluster edge. Make 42 contrasting colour spots. Fasten off and sew in yarn ends.

COLOURWAY
This design is worked with a main base colour which is used for the squares' final round, between the contrasting colours stripes in the rows and for the edging. Inner rounds of each motif are worked in a mix of single contrasting colours. Divide the number of squares by the number of contrasting colours to get an even colour mix. If you are following the sample, make six squares in each contrasting colour.

Instructions

SQUARE STRIPS
Using the main colour, join horizontal strips of seven squares together with the join-as-you-go technique (see page 65). If you are following the sample with seven contrast colour spots, use one spot of each colour in each strip when joining, mixing the order each time.

EDGE ROWS
Follow the cluster granny stitch extension instructions (see page 73) to add two rows to each side of each strip. Work in a contrasting colour and switch the contrasting colour for each side. Work different colours for each strip of squares.

A   Make six strips.
B   Lay the strips out to select the design order.
C   Omitting the top edge of the top strip and the bottom edge of the bottom strip, add a third row to each edge. Use the main colour and follow the cluster granny stitch extension Row 1.

JOIN THE STRIPS
Join a pair of strips together at a time and use a contrasting colour to join.

Strip 1
A   Join into the third chain (top of the last treble), work a row of cluster granny stitch extension Row 2 (see page 73).

Strip 2
B   Hold the strips back-to-back for the join-as-you-go method.
C   Treble into the top of the first treble stitch.
D   Double crochet between the trebles and the clusters of Strip 1 to join.
E   Continue along the row, using the join-as-you-go method.
F   Fasten off and sew in yarn ends.
G   Repeat the strips joining method, adding strips until all sections are joined. Total of six strips.

EDGING
Rows 1–2
A   Add two rows of cluster granny stitch extensions along the long edge of blanket, working in a different contrasting colour for each pair. Work clusters into gaps and into the space over the side of single trebles (3 chains).
B   Repeat on the opposite side.

Round 1
A   Add a final round along all edges in your main colour to complete the blanket. Follow the cluster granny stitch rounds instructions on page 72.
B   Fasten off.

FINISHING
A   Sew in any remaining ends.
B   Block if desired, following the instructions on page 74.

Top Tip

The join-as-you-go method used in this design can easily be switched for any joining method, just join the parts in the same places. Just repeat 'Join The Strips Step' on both pairs of strips before joining.

COLLAR

A collar is the perfect accessory to add that cute finishing touch to any outfit! Perfect to team with your favourite top or dress, this crochet collar is also great for dressing up a simple tee. Switch your squares and colourways for endless variations with a different look and feel. Why not make one for every outfit?!

YARN WEIGHT:
DK (light worsted)

HOOK SIZE:
4mm/US size G-6
(or to match tension)

TENSION:
One single square motif =
10 X 10cm (4 x 4in)

SIZE:
One size, widest point
across shoulders 39cm (15.¼in)

SAMPLE DESIGNS:
Main make: DK yarn,
Flower Square; worked in
three colours, one main colour
and two contrast colours.

DK variations: Flower Square;
worked in block colour and
mixed colours versions.

Aran variation: Sized up
on 4.5mm, Granny Square,
mixed colours.

APPROXIMATE METERAGE:
Total = 140m (154yd)

Main colour = 95m (104yd)

Contrasting colours =
45m (50yd)

TOTAL SQUARES:
Six.

Top Tip

Size your yarn up
to make a larger
statement collar,
perfect to team with
jackets and sweaters.

COLLAR
Step by Step Pattern Guide

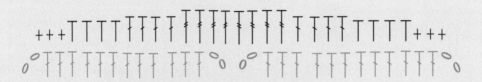

EDGE SHAPING STITCH SCHEMATIC

STEP 1 EDGE SHAPING

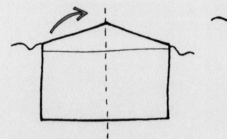

STEP 1 JOIN

STEP 1 JOIN FOLD OUT

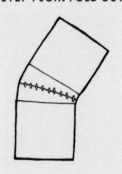

STEP 1 CONTINUE JOIN

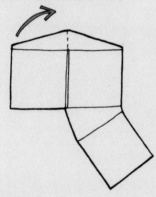

EDGING ROUND 1

EDGING ROUND 2

Getting Started

SQUARES:

Make six squares. Fasten off and sew in yarn ends. The sample design uses the Flower Square (page 45) but any square can be used.

COLOURWAY

If you are working in a colour mix, finish the final round in the main colour. This colour will also be used for joining and the infill panels that create the collar's curve.

Instructions

MAIN COLLAR

Using the main colour only, create the slope to form the curve of the collar and join the six squares for the collar.

Step 1

A   Take your first square, we are going to create the slope along the edge that forms the curve of the collar. Join in the main colour – the colour used for the square's last round – in to the top right corner space of a square with a double crochet.
B   Double crochet into the next 2 stitches.
C   Half treble into the next 4 stitches.
D   Treble into the next 4 stitches.
E   Double treble into the next 2 stitches.
F   Double treble 2 into the corner chain space.
G   Pick up your next square and continue the row along its edge.
H   Double treble 2 stitches into the corner chain space.
I   Double treble into the next 2 stitches.
J   Treble into the next 4 stitches.
K   Half treble into the next 4 stitches.
L   Double crochet into the next 3 stitches.
M   Leave your yarn end live, we will now join the two edges to create the triangular infill.
N   Fold the squares, right sides together.
O   Insert the hook through the first and last double crochets.
P   Using the double crochet joining method (page 63), work 1 double crochet ,through both layers, into each stitch along the sloped edge to join the pieces (15 double crochet stitches in total).
Q   Fasten off.

Step 2

A   Repeat step 1, starting on the opposite side of the square you have just joined and adding a new square.
B   Repeat until you have joined all six squares together in an arched formation.

EDGING

Round 1

A   Place your collar down in a U shape and, using the main colour, join into the central square's corner chain space with a slip stitch.
B   Chain 1 stitch.
C   Double crochet into each stitch and chain space of the edge until you reach the top corner chain space at the front opening.
D   Working into the corner chain space, (double crochet, chain, double crochet).
E   Double crochet into each stitch up to the next corner chain space.
F   Repeat step D, to get to the bottom edge of the collar.
G   Double crochet into each stitch along the edge of the square.
H   Double crochet into the corner chain space.
I   Double crochet 3 stitches over the side of the double treble post.
J   Double crochet into the top of each of the double treble stitches.
K   Double crochet 3 stitches over the side of the double treble post.
L   Repeat steps G–K four more times.
M   Double crochet into each stitch up to the corner chain space.
N   Working into the corner chain space, (double crochet, chain, double crochet).
O   Repeat steps M and N.
P   Double crochet into each stitch and chain space of the edge until you reach the first chain of the round.
Q   Join with a slip stitch into the first chain.
R   Fasten off if you're changing colour for the final round.

Round 2

A   Begin the round either by continuing with the main colour or by joining in a new colour with a slip stitch.
B   Chain 1.
C   Double crochet into each stitch up to the corner chain space.

D   Chain 61 stitches to form the foundation of the first tie.
E   Miss 1 stitch.
F   Slip stitch into the back bump of each of the 60 chain stitches to create the tie cord.
G   Double crochet back into the corner chain space.
H   Using the picot edge stitch (see page 66), work around the outside edge until you reach the opposite inside corner.
I   Double crochet in the corner chain space.
J   Chain 61 stitches to form the foundation of the second tie.

K   Miss 1 stitch.
L   Slip stitch into the back bump of each of the 60 chain stitches to create the second tie cord.
M   Double crochet back into the corner chain space.
N   Double crochet into each stitch until the first chain of the round.
O   Join with a slip stitch into the first chain.
P   Fasten off.

FINISHING
Sew in yarn ends and block your piece.

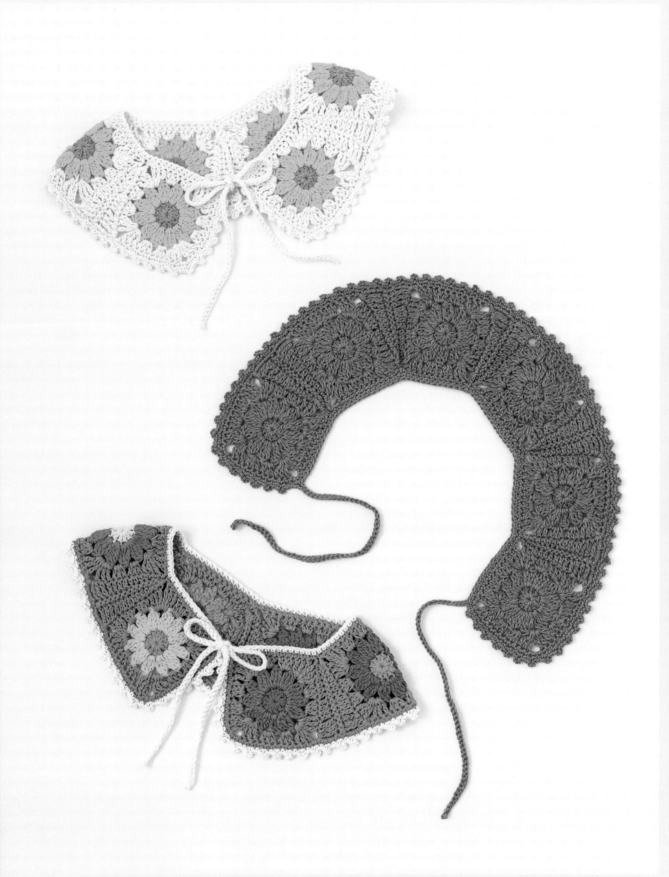

POUCH BAG

~~~~~~~~~~~~~~~~~~~~~

The perfect pouch bag to grace your wrist for fun-filled days! Made in crisp raffia this design holds its own, and it can easily be lined if that's your preference. Fill it up with all your must-have items and it take out for a twirl. This design whips up quickly so you can make one to match every party outfit you own!

YARN WEIGHT:
Aran (worsted)

HOOK SIZE:
4.5mm/US size 7
(or to match tension)

TENSION:
One extended square motif =
16 x 16cm (6¼ x 6¼in)

SIZE:
One size: circumference
64cm (25¼in); height
(excluding handle) 25cm (9¾in)

SAMPLE DESIGN:
Made with raffia yarn in two colours, worked alternating the colour each round.

APPROXIMATE METERAGE:
290m (318yd)

TOTAL SQUARES:
Five extended squares.

Getting Started

SQUARES
This design uses an extended square worked for six rounds. Make five six-round squares, fasten off and sew in ends. The sample design uses the Block Square, but any motif can be used. If you are not lining your bag a more solid square design works best.

COLOURWAY
The design is worked in two colours, alternating each round.
Round 1: Colour A
Round 2: Colour B
Round 3: Colour A
Round 4: Colour B
Round 5: Colour A

Top Tips

To line your bag, trace round the net, adding 1cm (⅜in) for seam allowances at the side seams and 2cm (¾in) to the top edges. The lining can be stitched up and then secured in place at the slip stitch row on the inside of the pouch. A lining will help floppier yarns keep the bag's shape and also allow you to use more open crochet designs if you wish.

POUCH BAG
Step by Step Pattern Guide

BAG BASE JOIN

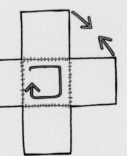

BAG SIDES JOIN

WORK BAG BODY EXTENSION ROUNDS, DRAWSTRING CHANNEL AND PICOT EDGE

STRAPS

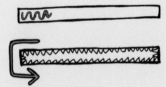

ATTACH STRAP AND WEAVE IN DRAWSTRING

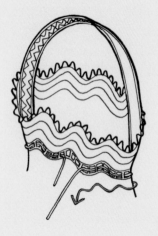

Instructions

BAG BODY

A Create a net of your bag. Join the four outer squares to the fifth, central square (bottom of bag) with a double crochet join (see page 63). Join on the wrong side of the work using colour B.

B Fold in and join the side edges with the double crochet join, working on the wrong side, to form a box shape which makes up the body of the bag.

BAG BODY EXTENSION ROUNDS
Round 1

Work along the open edge in colour B.

A Turn the bag the right way out, with joining seams on the inside.

B Join in with a slip stitch at any corner chain space.

C Chain 3 (counts as 1 treble), treble into the same space.

D Work 1 treble between each stitch, following the block stitch rows method (see page 73).

E At the last stitch, join with a slip stitch into the third chain from the start of the round to complete the round.

Round 2

On the inside of the round loosely work 1 slip stitch into each stitch of round. This creates a lip on the inside of your bag to attach the handle or a lining.

Round 3

A   Chain 1.
B   Working into the main edge, double crochet into the top of each stitch from Round 1.
C   Join with a slip stitch into the first chain.
D   Fasten off.

Round 4

This round creates the drawstring channel.

A   Using colour A, join in to any stitch with a slip stitch.
B   Chain 4 (this counts as first treble, 1 chain).
C   Miss 1 stitch.
D   Treble 1, chain 1 into next stitch.
E   Repeat steps C and D until last stitch.
F   Join with a slip stitch into the third chain from the start of the round to complete the round.
G   Fasten off.

Round 5

A   Using colour B, join into any chain space with a slip stitch.
B   Chain 3 (this counts as first treble).
C   Treble into the same space.
D   Treble 2 into each chain space of the round.
E   Join with a slip stitch into the third chain from the start of the round to complete the round.
F   Fasten off.

Round 6

A   Using colour A, join in between any stitch with a slip stitch.
B   Chain 3 (counts as 1 treble).
C   Work 1 treble between each stitch of the round.
D   Join with a slip stitch into the third chain from the start of the round to complete the round.
E   Fasten off.

Round 7

Repeat round 6 in colour B.

Round 8

Edge the final round in colour A working the picot stitch (see page 66).

HANDLE
Step 1

A   Using colour A, chain 6 + 1 turning chain.
B   Miss 1 stitch, double crochet into each stitch along chain (6 sts), turn work.
C   Continue working in rows, chain 1, double crochet back along the row until end.
D   Work double crochet for 54 rows in total (42cm [16½in]).
E   Fasten off.

Step 2

A   Using colour B, work the spike stitch edge around all sides of the handle.
B   Join in at the edge, 3 stitches and 3 rows in, working the spike stitch edging following the instructions on page 68.
C   In corners work (3 spike stitches, 1 chain, 3 spike stitches) into the same place to turn.
D   Stitches should line up with one another along both sides of the handle.
E   Fasten off.

FINISHING

A   Make a drawstring by making an 80cm (31½in) chain in colour A and slip stitching back across its entire length, working into the back bump of the stitch.
B   Thread the drawstring through the bag by weaving over and under the treble posts of Round 4.
C   Attach the handle to the slip stitch round on the inside of bag at either side. Use a double crochet or whip stitch join (see page 62).
D   Sew in all remaining yarn ends.

Top Tip

Use a chenille yarn for a luscious take on this design. Why not add beads or gems to make the perfect evening bag!

GRAPHIC GRID CUSHION

~~~~~~~~~~~~~~~~~~~~~~~~~

Mix or match? This cushion design matches the Graphic Grid Blanket (page 157), so you can choose to make a one-off piece or have it as part of a larger matching set! Designed to fit a 45cm (17¾in) cushion pad, this design is worked in a slightly tighter tension to the blanket to account for the stretch when it's padded out with a cushion pad.

Top Tips

If you want to use a large mix of colours, pull your design together by using one main colour for the final rounds of the squares and to mix into your border and joining rounds.

Work the border in cluster granny stitch (see page 72) for a different look and feel.

Adapt the size for larger cushions by adding further treble crochet border rounds.

YARN WEIGHT:
Chunky (bulky)

HOOK SIZE:
5.5mm/US size I-9
(or to match tension)

TENSION:
One single square motif = 13 x 13cm (5⅛ x 5⅛in)

SIZE:
One size, 43 x 43cm (17 x 17in) to fit a 45cm (17¾in) cushion pad

SAMPLE DESIGNS:
Two design variations, both worked in acrylic yarn.

Variation 1: Worked in eight colours, six colours for the squares and two colours for the border edging, to match the Graphic Grid Blanket.

Variation 2: Worked in Ferris Wheel Square design, with a mix of colours using black as a main colour.

APPROXIMATE METERAGE:
Total = 440m (482yd)

Square colours = 155m (170yd)

Border = 285m (312yd)

TOTAL SQUARES:
Eight.

GRAPHIC GRID CUSHION
Step by Step Pattern Guide

CENTRAL BLOCK AND BORDER ROUNDS, MAKE 2

JOIN, LEAVING ONE EDGE OPEN TO ADD CUSHION

COMPLETE DOUBLE CROCHET JOIN TO CLOSE

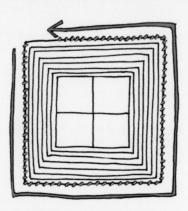

Getting Started

SQUARES

The squares in this project are joined together in groups of four, which then have outer rounds added. The cushion is made from two of these larger blocks, totalling eight individual squares. If you want the design to match the Graphic Grid Blanket design, follow the square layout illustrated on page 158. Fasten off the squares with a long tail (see page 61) for whip stitch and sew in all other remaining ends.

COLOURWAY

To follow the Graphic Grid colourway, use the colourway instructions on page 159. For the variation design use a random mix of colours in your square, finishing on a black final round. Use black for every third round of the border and for joining.

Instructions

DESIGN BLOCK

Make two.
A   Follow the instructions for the Graphic Grid Blanket design block until Border Round 2 (see page 159).
B   Repeat Border Round 2 four more times in your chosen colourway to increase the size.
C   Edge your square with double crochet following the Border Round 3 instructions. Fasten off with a short tail (see page 26).
D   Sew in all loose ends.

JOIN

Place your two blocks with wrong sides together and work on the right side of your work to join.
A   Working in your main colour, join into any corner chain space through both panels.
B   Chain 1.
C   Using the double crochet joining technique (see page 63), work around three sides of your square, leaving your yarn end live.
D   Insert your cushion pad through the opening to fill the crochet cover.
E   Pull the edges together and continue to crochet down the final side.
F   Join with a slip stitch into the first stitch to complete the round.
G   Fasten off leaving a 20cm (8in) tail.
H   Sew in the first part of the tail and tuck the rest inside the cushion. This long tail is left so that if you need to undo the cover and take out the cushion for any reason you have enough yarn to re-crochet the join easily.

GROOVY GRANNY BLANKET COAT

The Groovy Granny Blanket Coat is a hero piece that incorporates all five square designs. This make is just as perfect for bringing a blast of colour to a grey winter's day as it is for gracing the festival fields in the summer! This full-length coat is not a make for the faint hearted; it is a labour of love requiring many squares, but it's well worth it. If you decide to create a very colourful piece, make sure that you deal with your yarn ends as you go, otherwise it will add up to be a very long task at the end!

YARN WEIGHT:
DK (light worsted)

HOOK SIZE:
4mm/US size G-6
(or to match tension)

TENSION:
One single square motif =
10 x 10cm (4 x 4in)

SIZE:
XS–5XL, see chart

EASE:
30–45cm (12–18in) oversized fit

SAMPLE DESIGNS:
Two design variations, both worked in acrylic DK yarn:

Main make: Size L.
All five square designs used. All worked with the main colour (black) for the squares' last rounds. Fourteen contrasting colours are used for the inner rounds of the squares, colour changing every round, randomly mixed.

Variation: Size XL. Made with wider sleeves. Spot Squares and Granny Squares randomly mixed. Worked with the main colour (blue) used for one-colour Granny Squares and final rounds. Five contrasting colours used for spots and inner rounds of squares.

APPROXIMATE METERAGE
Total per square = 16.5m (18yd) with a long tail fasten off.

Main colour = 7m (7¾yd)

Contrasting colours = 9.5m (10½yd)

Total meterage is dependent on the size and length of coat made, see chart.

TOTAL SQUARES:
Will be determined by your chosen size, see chart.

GROOVY GRANNY BLANKET COAT
Step by Step Pattern Guide

JOIN BACK PANEL, REPEAT PROCESS ON BOTH FRONT PANELS

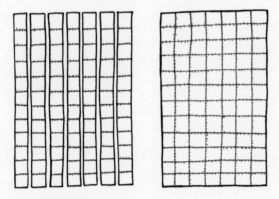

ADD ANY SIZING ROWS TO OUTER EDGES ON FRONT AND BACK PANELS

JOIN BLANKET COAT PANELS AND SLEEVES

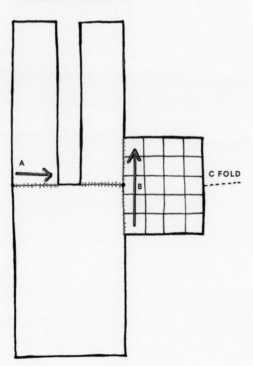

JOIN SLEEVES AND SIDE SEAMS ON BOTH SIDES

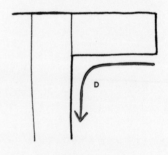

ADD LAPEL ROUNDS AND CUFF EDGING

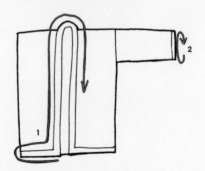

Getting Started

DESIGN METERAGE CALCULATIONS

The approximate meterage has been given for the maxi length coat. If you are shortening the coat, it's important to plan out your project to calculate any change in the yarn meterage required.

If you are making the full-length coat, be aware that it will 'drop' after a couple of wears. This means it will stretch slightly and hang lower than when you first finished and measured it. To make sure your garment doesn't become too long make it at least 10cm (4in) shorter than the maximum length you want.

Each square of this design uses 7m (7¾yd) of main colour (including join), and approximately 9.5m (10½yd) per square of contrasting colours. Use these figures to work out yarn usage if reducing the number of squares.

SQUARES

Follow the chart to make the correct number of squares for your coat. The sample design uses a mix of all the square designs. Fasten off your squares with a long tail (see page 61) for the double crochet joining method.

COLOURWAY

This design is worked with a main colour for the finals rounds of the squares, and for joining and extension rounds. A mix of colours is used for the inner rounds of the squares and lapel rounds. Inner rounds use a mix of 14 colours worked evenly in a random mix.

Instructions

BODY AND SLEEVE PANELS

A   Divide your squares between the panels for the back and front of the body and the panels for the sleeves.

B   Lay your squares out in the panels to make sure the colours and square patterns are distributed evenly.

C   Join your squares together into five panels (one for the back, two for the front and two for the sleeves) using the double crochet joining

technique (see page 63). First, join the short edges into vertical rows using the long tail fasten off yarn end, and then join the rows together using the main colour.

D   Fasten off and sew in all ends.

BODY SIZING ROWS

Refer to the chart to see if you need to add body sizing rows along the outer edges of your panels. Working only on the outside edges of the panels, along side seams only, add additional rows in the main colour using block stitch extension rows (see page 73).

COAT JOINING

A   Working in the main colour, join the top edge of the front panels to the back panel to create the shoulder seams. Place right sides together and work on the inside using the double crochet joining technique. Work from the outer edge inwards when joining, to ensure that the panels line up.

B   Now attach the sleeves to the joined body panels. Use stitch markers to line up the centre of your sleeve with the shoulder seam. Place right sides together and, working on the inside, join using the double crochet joining technique. Repeat for both sleeves.

C   To join sleeves and side seams: fold the garment in half along the shoulder seam, with right sides facing.

D   Using the double crochet joining technique, work along the sleeve edge from the cuff till you reach the body and continue joining, working all the way down to the bottom edge of the coat.

E   Fasten off.

F   Repeat steps D and E for the other side.

G   Sew in all joining ends.

LAPEL EDGING

Round 1

A   Working in the main colour, join in with a slip stitch in a corner chain space at the centre back.

B   Chain 3 (counts as 1 treble).

C   Treble between each stitch along the round, working 2 trebles into each chain space over joins, until corner (if working over treble extension rows, work 2 trebles over each treble post).

D (Treble 2, chain 2, treble 2) into corner
chain space.
E Repeat steps C and D up to the end
of the round.
F Join into the third chain with a slip stitch
to complete the round.
G Fasten off.

Round 2
A Join in a new colour with a slip stitch
between stitches at the centre back.
B Chain 3 (counts as 1 treble).
C Treble between each stitch along the round.
D (Treble 2, chain 2, treble 2) into corner
chain space.
E Repeat steps C and D up to the end
of the round.
F Join into the third chain with a slip stitch
to complete the round.
G Fasten off.

Rounds 3-5
Repeat Round 2 three more times changing
colour for each round.

Round 6
A Join in new colour with a slip stitch
in the top of a stitch at the centre back.
B Chain 1.
C Work one round of double crochet
edging (see page 67) to finish off.
D Fasten off and sew in yarn ends.

CUFF EDGING
Repeat for each cuff.

Round 1
A Working in the main colour, join in with
a slip stitch in a corner chain space
at the centre point under the cuff.
B Chain 3 (counts as 1 treble).
C Treble between each stitch, working
2 trebles into each chain space over joins.
D Join into the third chain with a slip stitch
to complete the round.

Rounds 2-4
A Chain 1.
B Work three rounds using the double
crochet edge technique (see page 67).
C Fasten off and sew in yarn ends.

Round 5
A Add spike stitch detailing to the edge
to finish. Follow the instructions for step 2
of the spike stitch edge on page 68.
B Fasten off and sew in yarn ends.

FINISHING
Use the instructions on page 74 to block
your piece.

Top Tips

Customise this design to suit you:
reduce the length to create a shorter
cardigan; widen the sleeves to make it
boxier; or remove the sleeves entirely to
make a long waistcoat. The possibilities
are endless! Plan your make to work
out how many squares you will need
to make the design perfect for you.

This is the perfect DK stash buster.
Pick a new main colour but work all
the inner rounds of your squares
in your odds and ends of yarn.

MEASUREMENTS			BODY			SLEEVES X 2	TOTAL SQUARES	APPROXIMATE METERAGE (YARDAGE)		
SIZE	FLAT CHEST WIDTH IN CM (IN)	LENGTH IN CM (IN)	FRONT X 2 SQUARES (W)	BACK SQUARES (W)	EDGE SIZING ROWS	SQUARES (D X L)		TOTAL	MAIN COLOUR SQUARE OUTER ROUND, JOINING, SIZING ROUNDS	CONTRAST COLOURS SQUARE INNER ROUNDS, CONTRAST EDGING
XS	50 (19¾)	115 (45¼)	2 x 11	5 x 11	–	4 x 4	131	2600 (2844)	1140 (1247)	1460 (1597)
S	56 (22)	115 (45¼)	2 x 11	5 x 11	+3	4 x 4	131	2800 (3062)	1330 (1455)	1470 (1608)
M	62 (24½)	115 (45¼)	2 x 11	5 x 11	+6	5 x 4	139	3145 (3440)	1590 (1739)	1555 (1700)
L	70 (27½)	125 (49¼)	3 x 12	7 x 12	–	5 x 4	196	3735 (4085)	1645 (1799)	2090 (2286)
XL	76 (30)	125 (49¼)	3 x 12	7 x 12	+3	5 x 3	186	3810 (4167)	1780 (1947)	2030 (2220)
2XL	82 (32¼)	125 (49¼)	3 x 12	7 x 12	+6	5 x 3	186	4035 (4413)	1995 (2182)	2040 (2231)
3XL	90 (35½)	125 (49¼)	4 x 12	9 x 12	–	5 x 3	234	4455 (4872)	1950 (2133)	2505 (2739)
4XL	96 (37¾)	125 (49¼)	4 x 12	9 x 12	+3	6 x 3	240	4780 (5228)	2210 (2417)	2570 (2811)
5XL	100 (39½)	125 (49¼)	4 x 12	9 x 12	+5	6 x 3	240	4930 (5392)	2355 (2576)	2575 (2816)

Top Tip

If you want to use a more open motif design, line your top. Use a stretchy fabric like jersey – you could even cut up an old t-shirt. Cut the fabric to size and whip stitch it to the crochet panel with a cotton thread.

TIE-BACK TOP

This tie-back top is a strappy summer number, perfect for beach holidays! The construction is a simple rectangle made from squares, worked with skinny straps that criss-cross the open back. The open corset-style back means this make is made with negative ease. The adjustable lacing means it fits you like a glove!

YARN WEIGHT:
DK (light worsted)

HOOK SIZE:
3.5mm/US size E-4
(or to match tension)

TENSION:
One single square motif =
8 x 8cm (3¼ x 3¼in)

SIZE:
XS–5XL, see chart

EASE:
Negative ease, tight fitting
with adjustable back ties

SAMPLE DESIGN:
A Block Square motif, made with DK cotton and worked on a small hook to produce a compact square. The main base colour is black with seven contrasting colours used for colour pops in Round 1 of the squares and for contrasting joining. Tight fitting with an open back and lace-up ties.

APPROXIMATE METERAGE:
Total meterage is dependent on size made, see chart.

Per square = 11.7m (12¾yd)

Main colour = 9.9m (10⅞yd)

Contrasting colours =
1.8m (2yd)

TOTAL SQUARES:
21–64 depending on
size made, see chart.

MEASUREMENTS			BODY	TOTAL SQUARES	APPROXIMATE METERAGE (YARDAGE)		
SIZE	BODY PANEL FLAT WIDTH IN CM (IN)	BODY LENGTH IN CM (IN)	SQUARES WIDTH X DEPTH		TOTAL	MAIN	CONTRAST
XS	58 (22¾)	26 (10¼)	7 x 3	21	335 (367)	260 (285)	75 (82)
S	66 (26)	26 (10¼)	8 x 3	24	380 (416)	295 (323)	85 (93)
M	74 (29¼)	26 (10¼)	9 x 3	27	420 (460)	325 (356)	95 (104)
L	82 (32¼)	26 (10¼)	10 x 3	30	460 (503)	355 (389)	105 (115)
XL	90 (35½)	32 (12½)	11 x 4	44	640 (705)	495 (541)	150 (164)
2XL	98 (38½)	32 (12½)	12 x 4	48	695 (760)	535 (585)	160 (175)
3XL	106 (41¾)	32 (12½)	13 x 4	52	755 (826)	580 (634)	175 (192)
4XL	122 (48)	32 (12½)	15 x 4	60	860 (941)	660 (722)	200 (219)
5XL	130 (51¼)	32 (12½)	16 x 4	64	915 (1001)	700 (766)	212 (235)

TIE-BACK TOP
Step by Step Pattern Guide

PIN SQUARE CORNERS TOGETHER
AND JOIN SHORT ROWS

WORK ALONG ADDING
MORE ROWS AND JOINING

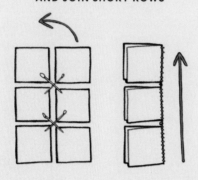

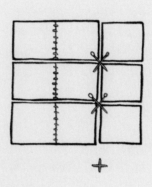

JOIN ALONG LONG STRIPS

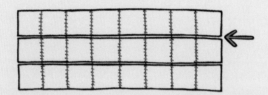

ADD BORDER ROUNDS
AND STRAPS

LACE UP THE BACK THROUGH
THE SQUARE CORNERS.

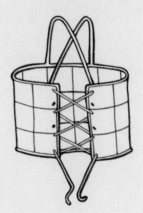

Getting Started

SQUARES:
The main sample uses the Block Square, but any motif can be used. Make the number of squares needed for the design. Fasten off and sew in yarn ends.

COLOURWAY
Main colour black is used along with seven contrasting colours as highlights. Work the first round of the squares in a contrasting colour and complete the square in the main colour. Contrasting colours are also used for joining and the edging round. Distribute the contrasting colours evenly.

Instructions

BODY
Join your squares together to make the body panel using the double crochet joining technique (see page 63).

A   Lay the squares out and distribute the different coloured centres evenly.
B   Use stitch markers or small safety pins to join the corners of the squares together while you join them. Pin the squares as you work, rather than pinning the whole piece at once.
C   Join the shorter rows first, alternating the colour for each join.
D   Then join the longer rows together, again, alternating the colour for each join.
E   Fasten off and sew in yarn ends.

EDGING
Double crochet around the edge of the body panel and add straps.

Round 1
A   Using a contrasting colour, join with a slip stitch into any corner stitch.
B   Chain 1.
C   Double crochet into each stitch along the edge.
D   In corner stitches (double crochet, chain, double crochet).
E   Repeat steps C and D until you reach the corner you started in.

F   Join into the first chain with a slip stitch to complete the round.
G   Fasten off.

Round 2
Repeat Round 1 in the main colour. Do not fasten off, keep the end live.

Round 3 (straps)
A   Using a stitch marker, mark the halfway point along the top of your panel. This is the centre of your top.
B   Using two more stitch markers, evenly mark each side of the centre where you wish your straps to be. A good guide is 10-16cm (4-6¼in) away from the centre point.
C   Continue the double crochet round, repeating Round 1 until you reach the stitch marker.
D   At the first marker, chain a length of 140cm (55in).
E   Miss the first stitch of the chain, and double crochet into the back bump of each chain stitch.
F   Double crochet anchor into the next stitch of the body panel.
G   Double crochet into each stitch until the next stitch marker.
H   Repeat steps E and F for the second strap.
I   Continue to double crochet, repeating Round 1 until the end.
J   Fasten off and sew in ends.

FINISHING
A   Block the body panel, following the instructions on page 74.
B   Lace up the back panel by crisscrossing the ties using the corner chain spaces of the edge squares as eyelets.

Top Tip

For a different feel, why not switch the crochet straps for ribbons. Skip Round 3 and add another round of double crochet to finish off. Cut your ribbons to the same length as the crochet straps and sew in place.

SWEATER VEST

~~~~~~~~~~

Pack a punch with this wardrobe favourite! This classic sweater vest is a transitional piece that's great for between seasons or for layering. It works up brilliantly in either a woolly yarn for the winter months or in cool cotton for the summer season. Plus, the deep arm holes make this design perfect to pair with billowy sleeves!

YARN WEIGHT:
Aran (worsted)

HOOK SIZE:
4.5mm/US size 7
(or to match tension)

TENSION:
One single square motif
(XS–XL) = 11.5 x 11.5cm
(4½ x 4½in)

One single square motif +
1 round
(2XL–5XL) = 14 x 14cm
(5½ x 5½in)

Smaller three-round square
(for sleeves) = 8 x 8cm
(3⅛ x 3⅛in)

SIZE:
XS–5XL, see chart

EASE:
No ease, tight fitting

SAMPLE DESIGNS:
Two design variations:

Main make: Sizes M and 3XL.
Worked in cotton aran using
Granny, Ferris Wheel and
Flower Square designs. Main
colour white and a mix of seven
contrasting colours changing
every round, randomly mixed.

Variation: Size L. Made in aran
wool in the Granny Square
motif. Main colour black and
eight contrasting colours
changing every round,
randomly mixed.

APPROXIMATE METERAGE:
Total meterage is dependent
on the size made, see chart.

TOTAL SQUARES:
Body = 18 full motifs with
rounds added for sizing, see
chart. Side panels and straps =
nine to 18 smaller three-round
squares, total will vary
depending on size, see chart.

SWEATER VEST
Step by Step Pattern Guide

JOIN BODY PANELS X 2

WORK BODY BORDER EDGING ROUNDS

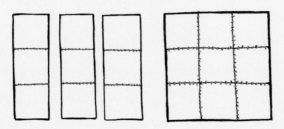

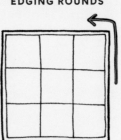

JOIN STRAPS X 2

JOIN SIDE PANELS X 2 AND ADD BORDER ROUNDS

JOIN TOGETHER ALL PANELS

FINISH VEST BY ADDING NECK, ARM AND BOTTOM EDGING

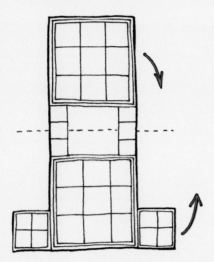

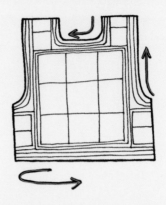

Getting Started

SQUARES

This design uses a mix of full-size motifs and smaller squares. Full-size squares are used for the body panels: the sample uses a mix of the Granny, Ferris Wheel, and Flower Squares, but any square design can be used. For sizes 2XL–5XL make your main squares one round larger.

Each Body panel includes:

- Granny Square x 3
- Flower Square x 4
- Ferris Wheel x 2

Make 18 full-size squares. Finish them off with a long tail fasten off (see page 61), ready to join with the double crochet joining method (see page 63).

The small squares are used for the straps and side panels. The number of squares needed depends on the size of garment you are making, see the chart on page 141. Smaller squares are worked for three rounds in the Granny pattern. Finish off your small squares with a long tail fasten off, ready to join with the open crochet joining method (see page 64).

COLOURWAY

Use a mix of colours for your squares, changing colour each round, and work the final round of each square with the main colour. The border and edging rounds mix contrasting colours with the main colour for an even colour spread. To work out contrasting colour quantities use the chart on page 140. Divide the total approximate meterage for your colour by the number of colours you wish to use.

Instructions

BODY PANELS

A   Make two panels for the body using the full-size motifs. Join the panels with a double crochet join. Join the short edges together into strips using the yarn from the long tail fasten off. Then use the main colour to join the long edges of the strips. Add border edging rounds to size, following the chart for the total number of additional rounds.

B   Make two side panels of smaller, three-round Granny Squares. Use the chart to determine how many squares are needed in each panel. Join the short edges of the squares together using long the tail from fastening off with the open crochet joining technique. Then use the main colour to join the strips together (if you have multiple strips).

C   Make two straps of smaller, three-round Granny Squares. Join the short edges of the squares together using the long tail from fastening off with the open crochet join.

BORDER ROUNDS

Add border rounds to the body, side panels and strap panels to the appropriate size – follow the chart for the number of additional rounds needed. Work the first border round in the main colour and alternate contrasting colours for any subsequent rounds.

JOINING PANELS

A   Join the side and strap panels to the body panel using the open crochet join. Work in a colour that matches one of the edges for an invisible join.

B   When joining, work from the outside edge inwards. At the last corner chain space along the join edge of the side/strap panels work one join into the corner chain space, chain 3 and work into the corner space again joining in the next body space. This last join helps with shaping of the neck and under arm.

NECK AND ARM EDGING:

Repeat Rounds 1–3 on the neck and both arm holes.

Round 1

A   Using the main colour, join with a slip stitch into the gap at the centre of the underarm for the sleeve edging, and at the top of the shoulder for the neck edging.

B   Chain 3 (counts as 1 treble), 2 treble crochets into the same space.

C   Work 3 trebles into each gap up to the joining point (3 trebles count as 1 cluster).

D   At right angle join points (corner chain space and next space), treble 1 into each gap. This helps with shaping in the next round.

E   Continue working 1 cluster into each gap until the next right angle join point, repeat step D.

F   Continue working steps D and E until you complete the round.

G Slip stitch into the third chain from the beginning of the round.

Round 2

A Chain 3 (counts as 1 treble).
B Work 1 cluster into each gap until you reach the space before your single corner trebles.
C Work 1 cluster between your two corner trebles, miss the next gap.
D Repeat steps B and C until you complete the round.
E In the first space, treble 2 to complete the round.
F Slip stitch into the third chain from the beginning to complete the round.
G Fasten off

Edging Round:

A Join with a slip stitch into the gap at the centre of the underarm for the sleeve edging, and at the top of the shoulder for the neck edging.
B Chain 1, double crochet into each stitch.
C Slip stitch into the first chain from the beginning of the round.
D Fasten off.

BOTTOM EDGING

Round 1:

A Using the main colour, join with a slip stitch into the bottom edge at the side of garment.
B Chain 3 (counts as 1 treble), 2 trebles into the same space.
C Work 1 granny cluster into each gap along the edge, including corner chain spaces at panel joins.
D Slip stitch into the third chain from the beginning of the round.

Round 2

A Chain 3 (counts as 1 treble).
B Treble 2 into the same gap.
C Work 1 granny cluster into the next gap and into each gap of the round.
D Slip stitch into the third chain from the beginning of the round to complete the round.

Round 3

A Chain 1, double crochet into each stitch of the round.
B Slip stitch into the first chain from the beginning of the round.
C Fasten off and sew in yarn ends.

Top Tips

Extend the final vest into a pinafore dress by repeating Rounds 1 and 2 of the bottom edging until your vest is the desired length, changing colour as you desire.

Work up in a dark main colour and wool yarn for a winter take on the sweater vest. Use the Granny Square for a timeless classic! If you are using squares with a cluster edge, like the Granny Square, remember to join with an open crochet join.

SIZE	TOTAL METERAGE (YARDAGE)	MAIN COLOUR	CONTRAST COLOUR
XS	570 (624)	310 (339)	260 (285)
S	625 (684)	365 (399)	260 (285)
M	710 (777)	375 (410)	335 (367)
L	745 (815)	405 (443)	340 (372)
XL	830 (908)	415 (454)	415 (454)
2XL	960 (1050)	510 (558)	450 (492)
3XL	1150 (1258)	515 (564)	635 (694)
4XL	1230 (1345)	515 (563)	715 (782)
5XL	1340 (1466)	520 (569)	820 (897)

MEASUREMENTS			BODY				SIDES AND STRAPS – SMALLER THREE-ROUND SQUARES					
SIZE	FLAT CHEST WIDTH IN CM (IN)	LENGTH IN CM (IN)	SQUARE EXTENSION ROUNDS	BODY X 2 SQUARES (WXD)	TOTAL SQUARES	BODY PANEL BORDER EXTENSION ROUNDS	SIDE X 2 SQUARES (WXD)	SIDE PANEL EXTENSION ROUNDS	STRAP X 2 SQUARES (WXD)	STRAP PANEL EXTENSION ROUNDS	TOTAL SQUARES SMALLER THREE-ROUND SQUARE
XS	41 (16⅛)	47 (18½)	–	3 x 3	18	–	1 x 2	+1	1 x 3	–	10
S	44 (17⅓)	49 (19¼)	–	3 x 3	18	+1	1 x 2	+1	1 x 3	–	10
M	49 (19¼)	51 (20)	–	3 x 3	18	+2	1 x 2	+2	1 x 3	–	10
L	54 (21¼)	51 (20)	–	3 x 3	18	+2	2 x 2	+1	1 x 3	–	14
XL	58 (22¾)	54 (21¼)	+1	3 x 3	18	+3	2 x 2	+2	1 x 3	–	14
2XL	62 (24½)	58 (22¾)	+1	3 x 3	18	+1	2 x 3	+1	1 x 3	+1	18
3XL	68 (26¾)	62 (24½)	+1	3 x 3	18	+3	2 x 3	+2	1 x 3	+1	18
4XL	72 (28¼)	64 (25¼)	+1	3 x 3	18	+4	2 x 3	+2	1 x 3	+1	18
5XL	76 (30)	66 (26)	+1	3 x 3	18	+5	2 x 3	+3	1 x 3	+1	18

SCARF

A chunky statement scarf, this project is perfect for practising your squares! The chunky yarn works up quickly, meaning this is a project that provides almost instant gratification. It's a great beginners' project as the thick yarn is helpful for getting used to the stitches. The chunky outcome will also keep you warm all winter long!

YARN WEIGHT:
Super chunky (super bulky)

HOOK SIZE:
10mm/US size N-15
(or to match tension)

TENSION:
One single square motif =
22 x 22cm (8¾ x 8¾in)

SIZE:
One size: 285cm (112in) long
by 22cm (8¾in) wide

SAMPLE DESIGN:
Worked in super chunky
wool mix yarn. Two of each
of the five square designs,
eight colours, worked in
a random mix.

APPROXIMATE METERAGE:
Total = 440m (482yd)

TOTAL SQUARES:
Ten.

Top Tips

Size down your yarn and
hook to make the scarf
in a smaller size.

Make multiple scarfs and
join strips together to
make a chunky blanket.

SCARF
Step by Step Pattern Guide

WHIP STITCH
JOINING

FRINGING

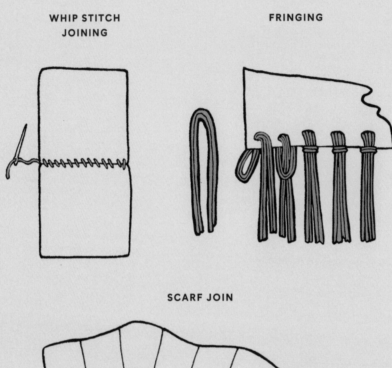

SCARF JOIN

Getting Started

SQUARES
Make 10 squares, two of each motif pattern. Fasten the squares off with the long tail fasten off (see page 61) for whip stitch.

COLOURWAY
Eight colours, change colour each round and mix the colours evenly.

Instructions

JOINING
A   Decide on the order of your squares, balancing the mix of colours and motifs.
B   Line your squares up with the yarn tails in the top right corner.
C   Whip stitch (see page 62) your first two squares together using the long yarn tail and joining them from the top edge.
D   Repeat until you have joined all your squares.

FRINGE
A   Cut your leftover yarn into equal lengths to make a fringe of your desired size. The yarn lengths will be folded in half when threaded through the scarf edge, so take this into account when cutting them.
B   Taking two strands at a time, fold the yarn lengths in half and pull the centre of the lengths through a stitch to make a loop.
C   Pull the ends of the fringe through the loop and pull to tighten. This makes a lark's head knot.
D   Repeat in each stitch of both ends of the scarf to complete the fringing.

FINISHING
Sew in the yarn ends and trim the fringe so that it is all the same length.

BERET

Transform your squares into a circle and create your own patchwork beret! Let this hat be the cherry on top of all your favourite outfits. This project is worked in a tight tension on a small hook to give body and structure to the hat.

YARN WEIGHT:
DK (light worsted)

HOOK SIZE:
2.5mm /US size B-1 or C-2 (or to match tension) for main body of beret and 3mm /US size D (or size up) for the headband

TENSION:
One single square motif = 7 x 7cm (2¾ x 2¾in). Tension is purposefully tight to make a dense fabric

SIZE:
One size, approximately 28cm (11in) in diameter when flat and to fit head size 54–58cm (21¼–22¾in)

SAMPLE DESIGN:
Acrylic yarn, worked in Granny Sqaures in nine colours, one main colour and eight contrasting colours.

APPROXIMATE METERAGE:
Total = 290m (318yd)

Main colour = 175m (192yd)

Contrasting colours = 115m (126yd)

TOTAL SQUARES:
24

Top Tips

This design works best in a woolly yarn (acrylic or natural) so that it has body and keeps its shape. It would also look fantastic in a fluffy yarn like mohair.

DK yarns can range slightly in their thickness from brand to brand, this design works best with yarn that sits on the thinner side of the DK range to help get the correct tension.

BERET
Step by Step Pattern Guide

JOIN

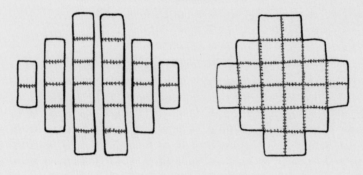

CORNER FOLDS

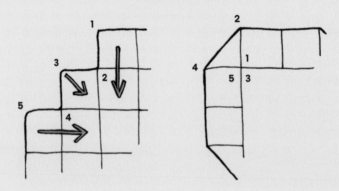

CORNER JOINS

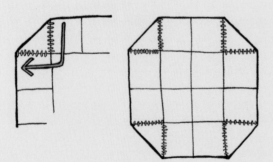

INNER HEADBAND

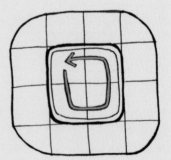

Getting Started

SQUARES

Make 24 squares. Fasten the squares off with the long tail fasten off (see page 61) for double crochet. The sample design uses the Granny Square, but any motif can be used. Tension for this make is important, if your squares are even just a little bit larger it can increase the size of the final make dramatically.

COLOURWAY

Start with your contrasting colour and use the main colour on every other row.

Instructions

JOINING

A   Following the diagram, lay the squares out in the diamond shape shown in the illustration. Position the squares with the long tails at the top right and in your desired pattern of colours.

B   Join the squares using the double crochet joining technique (see page 63). Work in vertical rows first, joining the short edges.

C   Join the longer sides together to complete the base.

D   Sew in the ends and lightly block the beret base.

E   Using the illustration as a guide, fold points 1, 3 and 5 into the centre with the right sides facing to create a circular shape.

F   Use a stitch marker to connect the three folded corners and to hold them in place while you join. Do the same for each side.

G   Join each corner separately. Starting at the inside corner (point 2), join along the edge with double crochet, working towards the outside point (point 1).

H   Double crochet through the corner of the central square, joining points 3 and 1 together. Work though the same central square corner again, joining points 3 and 5 together.

I   Double crochet inwards between points 5 and 4, along the remaining two open edges.

J   Fasten off in the last corner chain space.

K   Repeat steps H to K on the three remaining corners to complete the body of the beret.

L   Give the hat a second blocking and ease it into a circular shape.

INNER HEADBAND

Round 1

A   Work in the 3mm (or larger) hook size for the headband.

B   Join in at a stitch halfway along any square, chain 2.

C   Half treble around the inner edge of the beret. This round also includes decreases to help create the curved shape. Between the squares in the joined corners, half treble 2 together, by working the first part of the stitch in one space and the second part of the stitch over the join in the next to decrease.

D   At the corner points, half treble 2 together, working in points 1 and 5 and skipping point 3.

E   Work an entire round following steps C and D.

F   Join with a slip stitch into the 2nd chain to complete the round.

Rounds 2–4

A   Chain 1.

B   Double crochet into each stitch.

C   Join with a slip stitch into the 1st chain to complete the round.

D   Repeat steps A to C twice more.

Round 5

A   Using a loose slip stitch, work into each stitch of the final round to help ensure that the hat does not stretch out of shape. Do not do this too tightly as it will reduce the head size.

B   Fasten off and sew in any remaining ends.

Top Tip

To create a peplum top,
follow the dress join
instructions but make the
dress skirt only one row of
squares deep. Join both parts
and edge the top using the top
bottom edge instructions.

SUMMER SQUARES TOP AND SKIRT SET

A summer number to make your own! This pattern can be used in multiple ways: create a crop top and skirt that can be worn as a set or as separates; work the parts together to create a dress, customising the length to suit you; or use the pattern to make a top with a peplum. This piece is a labour of love that is worked in fine yarn on a 2.5mm hook for a lightweight feeling fabric. The pattern can be worked in so many ways, so grab your colouring pencils and squared paper and start planning the perfect design for you.

YARN WEIGHT:
Fine/3 ply/4 ply (fingering/sock/sport)

HOOK SIZE:
2.5 mm/US size B-1 or C-2 (or to match tension)

TENSION:
One single square motif = 7 x 7cm (2¾ x 2¾in)

SIZE:
XS–5XL, see chart

EASE
No ease, tight fitting

SAMPLE DESIGNS:
Two design variations:

Main make: Skirt and top in size S. Worked in mercerised cotton using the Block Square and the double crochet joining technique (see page 63). Worked in eight colours with a contrasting edge and join colour.

Variation: Peplum top in size L. Worked in cotton using the Granny Square and the join as you go method (see page 65). Worked in seven colours with a contrasting edge and join colour.

APPROXIMATE METERAGE:
10.3m (11yd) per square, dependant on your chosen design

TOTAL SQUARES:
Will be determined by your chosen size. Work out the total by using the chart and planning your design if you are customising.

SUMMER SQUARES TOP AND SKIRT SET
Step by Step Pattern Guide

JOIN TOP BODY PANEL

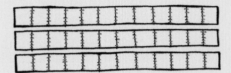 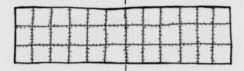

JOIN STRAPS X 2   JOIN TOP SIDES AND MARK AND JOIN STRAPS

 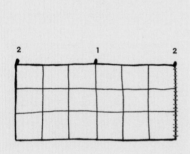 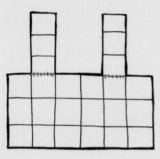

WORK NECK, STRAP AND BOTTOM EDGING

CONSTRUCT SKIRT AND ADD WAISTBAND AND BOTTOM EDGING. MAKE WAIST TIE AND THREAD THROUGH

DRESS JOIN, WORK BOTH PARTS TOGETHER AT WAISTBAND

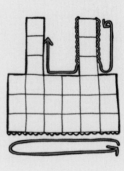 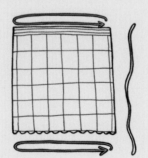 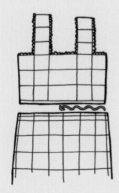

Getting Started

DESIGN METERAGE CALCULATIONS

The approximate meterage has been given for the crop top and mini skirt in the charts on page 155. If you are lengthening the skirt or adapting the pattern in any way, it's important to plan your project out to calculate any change in the yarn meterage required. Each square uses 10.3m (11yd) of the main colour, and approximately 1.2m (1yd) of the contrasting colour per square to join with the double crochet join. Use these figures to work out yarn usage for any additional squares.

SQUARES

Follow the chart to make the correct number of squares for your size. Fasten off squares and sew in the centre ends. Most outer ends can be trapped in the stitches when joining. Any remaining yarn ends can be sewn in at the end of the make. The main sample design uses the Block Square, but any motif can be used.

COLOURWAY

Eight colours are used alongside a black edging and border. Work the squares in a block colour. Divide the total number of squares by the number of colours used for an even spread.

Instructions

CROP TOP
Construct and join

Use the chart to calculate the number of squares needed and their layout.

A Lay out your design.
B Use the contrasting joining colour and the double crochet join (see page 63) to join the short edges of the squares together to create long strips.
C Join the long strips together to form the top panel.
D Join the two short edges of the panel together to create the body tube section of the top.
E Join the two strips of strap squares together using the same method as for the body.
F Lay the body tube flat.
G Using stitch markers mark the centre of the body tube, mark the first centre point at a joining seam. This will become the centre front or back of your top (point 1).
H Mark the opposing centre point by folding the body tube at this point. This won't always fall on a seam, it may also be at the centre of a square (point 1).
I Position the top so that the two central stitch markers are touching, this now indicates the front and back.
J Use stitch markers to note the side points, these indicate the underarms (point 2). You have now marked out four points on your top.
K Place the straps along the top edge, position them centrally between points 1 and 2. Attach the straps using the double crochet join.

NECK AND STRAPS EDGING

Working in the contrasting joining colour, add picot edging to your top edges, working over both the neck and straps.

A Join in at a shoulder point with a slip stitch.
B Chain 1.
C Work into each stitch following the picot edge instructions (see page 66). When working the picot stitch pattern over the top edge of the neck and underarms, only work into stitches, skip working into the corner chain spaces at the joins.
D Slip stitch into the first chain from the beginning of the round and fasten off.

BOTTOM EDGE

Use the contrasting joining colour.

Round 1
A Join into any cluster gap with a slip stitch.
B Chain 3 (counts as 1 treble).
C Treble 1, chain 1 into the same space you joined in.
D (Treble 2, chain 1) into the next and each cluster gap and corner chain space of the round.
E Slip stitch into the third chain from the beginning to complete the round.
F Fasten off.

Round 2
A Chain 1.
B Edge the final round in picot edging.
C Slip stitch into the first chain from the beginning and fasten off.
D Sew in any remaining yarn ends.

SKIRT

Construct and Join

Use the chart to calculate the number of squares for the width of your skirt. Work to the skirt length of your planned design.

A Lay out your design.
B Work the short edges of your squares together to create long strips.
C Join your long strips together to form your skirt panel.
D Join the two edges of the panel together to create the skirt.

WAISTBAND

Work the waistband in contrasting joining yarn.

Round 1

To shape the waistband for sizes XS–3XL use stitch markers to mark five square corner joins evenly spaced around the top edge of the skirt. You will work fewer stitches at these spaces to shape the waistband and to match up both garments. For sizes 4XL and 5XL there is no need to decrease over these stitches.

A Join into any cluster gap with a slip stitch.
B Chain 3 (counts as 1 treble).
C Treble 1, chain 1 into the same space you joined in.
D (Treble 2, chain 1) into each cluster gap and corner chain space along the edge up to the stitch marker.
E At the marked corner chain space, work 1 treble into next two corner chain spaces, chain 1.
F Repeat steps D and E until the end of the round.
G Slip stitch into the third chain from the beginning to complete the round.

Round 2

A Chain 4 (counts as 1 treble, 1 chain).
B (Treble 2, chain 1) into the next and each cluster gap of the round.
C Treble 1 into the first gap.
D Slip stitch into the third chain from the beginning to complete the round.

Round 3

A Chain 3 (counts as 1 treble).
B Treble 1, chain 1 into the same space you joined in.
C (Treble 2, chain 1) into the next and each cluster gap of the round.
D Slip stitch into the third chain from the beginning to complete the round.
E Fasten off.

TIE

A Make a chain: the chain length should measure 1.5 times the circumference of the waist.
B Working back along the chain, slip stitch into the back hump each of stitch to create a tie cord.
C Fasten off, sew in the ends of the tie cord.
D Working from the centre front through Round 3, weave the tie under and over the treble clusters in chain spaces to create a drawstring.

BOTTOM EDGING

Add picot edging in the contrasting joining colour. Work into each stitch of the bottom edge.

FINISHING

Block if desired, following the instructions on page 74.

DRESS JOIN

These two separate garments can easily be joined together to create a dress.

1 Follow the instructions for the top, omitting the final picot round at the bottom edge.
2 Follow the instructions for the skirt up to Waist Band Round 2.
3 Check that there are the same number of clusters around the bottom edge of the top and the top edge of the skirt, as these need to match up.

Waistband Round 3 (join)

Use the join-as-you-go method (see page 65) to join both pieces together.

A Turn both the skirt and the top inside out so that you are working on the wrong side.
B Chain 3 (counts as 1 treble).
C Holding the edges of both pieces together with right sides facing, double crochet into a cluster gap of the top (right side).
D Treble 2 into the next cluster gap of the skirt (wrong side).
E Double crochet into the next cluster gap of the top to anchor them together (right side).
F Repeat steps D and E until you have worked in each cluster gap of the round.
G Treble into the first cluster gap of the skirt, where you started the round.
H Slip stitch into the third chain from the beginning to complete the round.
I Fasten off.
J Turn the work right side out.

TIE

Follow the skirt tie instructions.

Top Tip

If using a cluster-edged square,this design is perfect for the join as you go technique. Use this method to create your strips, make three-round squares and use the join as you go method to work the final round in a new colour. Join the longer strips together with a double crochet open join.

MEASUREMENTS			TOP			CROP TOP TOTAL APPROXIMATE METERAGE (YARDAGE)	
SIZE	CHEST CIRCUMFERENCE IN CM (IN)	TOP LENGTH IN CM (IN)	CROP TOP SQUARES (W X L)	STRAPS X 2 SQUARES (L)	TOTAL SQUARES	SQUARE COLOUR	JOIN AND EDGING
XS	77 (30¼)	39 (15¼)	11 x 3	5	43	445 (487)	100 (110)
S	84 (33)	39 (15¼)	12 x 3	5	46	475 (519)	105 (115)
M	98 (38½)	46 (18⅛)	14 x 4	5	66	680 (744)	135 (148)
L	105 (41⅓)	46 (18⅛)	15 x 4	5	70	725 (793)	140 (153)
XL	112 (44)	49 (19¼)	16 x 4	6	76	785 (858)	155 (170)
2XL	126 (49½)	49 (19¼)	18 x 4	6	84	870 (951)	170 (186)
3XL	133 (52½)	49 (19¼)	19 x 4	6	88	910 (995)	175 (191)
4XL	147 (57⅘)	52.5 (20¾)	21 x 4	7	98	1010 (1105)	195 (213)
5XL	154 (60½)	52.5 (20¾)	22 x 4	7	102	1055 (1154)	210 (230)

MEASUREMENTS			SKIRT		SKIRT TOTAL APPROXIMATE METERAGE (YARDAGE)	
SIZE	HIPS CIRCUMFERENCE IN CM (IN)	SKIRT LENGTH IN CM (IN)	SKIRT SQUARES (W X D)	TOTAL SQUARES	SQUARE COLOUR	JOIN AND EDGING
XS	84 (33)	46 (18⅛)	12 x 6	72	745 (815)	145 (159)
S	91 (35¾)	46 (18⅛)	13 x 6	78	805 (880)	155 (170)
M	105 (41⅓)	46 (18⅛)	15 x 6	90	930 (1017)	180 (197)
L	112 (44)	46 (18⅛)	16 x 6	96	990 (1083)	190 (208)
XL	119 (46¾)	46 (18⅛)	17 x 6	102	1055 (1154)	200 (219)
2XL	133 (52½)	46 (18⅛)	19 x 6	114	1175 (1285)	225 (246)
3XL	140 (55)	46 (18⅛)	20 x 6	120	1240 (1356)	235 (257)
4XL	147 (58)	46 (18⅛)	21 x 6	126	1300 (1422)	245 (268)
5XL	154 (60½)	46 (18⅛)	22 x 4	132	1360 (1487)	260 (285)

GRAPHIC GRID BLANKET

The Graphic Grid blanket adds a bold twist to the traditional square quilt, and it's made using chunky yarn, so it works up quickly for its size. It is constructed in large blocks that are joined together; each block contains four squares in the centre that are edged with border rounds. The possibilities for colour combinations and motif mixes in this project are endless; follow along with the sample or mix and match your own!

Top Tips

You can easily size this make down by reducing the number of blocks or by working in a thinner yarn.

Work the border in cluster granny stitch for a different look and feel (see page 72).

Different colourways and square choices will change this blanket dramatically, why not try the Ferris Wheel Square (see page 49) used for the Graphic Grid Cushion (see page 123).

YARN WEIGHT:
Chunky (bulky)

HOOK SIZE:
6mm/US size J-10
(or to match tension)

TENSION:
One single square motif =
14 x 14cm (5½ x 5½in)

SIZE:
One size, 155 x 155cm (61 x 61in)

SAMPLE DESIGN:
Acrylic yarn. Worked in Spot Squares and Block Squares in eight colours, six colours for the squares and two colours for the border edging.

APPROXIMATE METERAGE:
Total = 2,380m (2,603yd)

Square colours =
1,370m (1,498yd)

Border main colour =
650m (711yd)

Contrast border colour =
360m (394yd)

TOTAL SQUARES:
64

GRAPHIC GRID BLANKET
Step by Step Pattern Guide

DESIGN AND COLOURWAY A

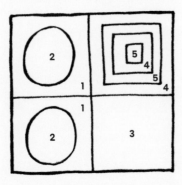

DESIGN AND COLOURWAY B

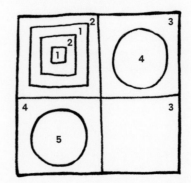

CENTRAL BLOCK JOIN, MAKE 16

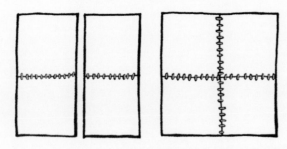

ADD BORDER ROUNDS

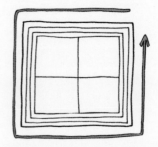

JOIN IN STRIPS

JOIN STRIPS AND EDGE

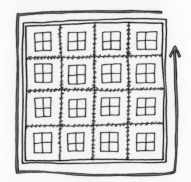

Getting Started

SQUARES

The squares in this project are joined together in groups of four, which then have outer rounds added. The blanket has a total of 16 of these larger blocks, totalling 64 individual squares. For the sample design each block contains: two Spot Squares, a Granny Square, and a Block Square, but any squares could be used. Fasten off the squares with a long tail (see page 61) for whip stitch and sew in all other remaining ends.

Make one large block at a time as this will allow you to plan out your design as you work on this larger project. The design is made up of two motif combinations in a mix of colourways, see the illustration for the layout of the squares. To follow the sample, make half of your larger blocks in style A and half in style B, alternate these in your blanket layout.

COLOURWAY

The squares are worked in a mix of six colours. The larger blocks are edged in two contrasting colours, one of which is also used to join all the larger blocks together. This will be referred to as the 'main colour' in the pattern. The individual squares are worked in a block colour, or a monochrome colour mix to create a graphic pattern. Take care to distribute your colours evenly across the square designs. The numbers on the layout illustration refer to the colour blocking.

Instructions

DESIGN BLOCK
Repeat 16 times for each large block.

Joining the central block
Join four motifs together with whip stitch (see page 62).

A   Using the long tails left after fastening off, first join the two sets of two squares. Place the short edges together to create two vertical rows of two squares.
B   Now join both rows together using whip stitch. If you want this join to be discreet, use the colour of the square edge.
C   Sew in yarn ends and fasten off.

Border Round 1
A   Start with the main colour on your hook.
B   Follow the block stitch border Round 1 instructions on page 72 to complete the round.

Border Round 2
A   Start with the next colour on your hook.
B   Follow the Block Square increase instructions on page 37 to complete the round.

Border Round 3
A   Start with the main colour on your hook.
B   Join into any corner chain space.
C   Chain 2, double crochet into same corner space.
D   Work 1 double crochet in-between each stitch along the edge.
E   (Double crochet, chain, double crochet) in corner chain space.
F   Repeat steps D and E until you reach the first chain of the round.
G   Join into the first chain with a slip stitch.
H   Fasten off with a long tail for a double crochet join (see page 63).

JOIN
Using your main colour, join 16 large blocks together in four rows of four using the double crochet joining technique.
A   Lay out your large blocks in the shape of the blanket and arrange them with the long tails positioned at the top right of each block.
B   Join the short edges together first to create four strips.
C   Join the strips together along the long edges to create the blanket.

EDGING
Using your main colour, work two rounds of double crochet as an edging.
A   Join in at any corner chain space.
B   Chain 1.
C   Follow the in instructions for the double crochet edge for two rounds (see page 67).

FINISHING
Sew in any remaining yarn ends and block.

TOTE BAG

We all have canvas tote bags that have started to look a bit sad after a few uses. Why not give them a new and colourful lease of life by covering them with crochet?

Getting Started

SQUARES:
Measure your tote bag and calculate the number of whole squares needed to cover each side. The sample tote bag was 41 x 37cm (16⅛ x 14½in), so it needed 12 squares per side, a total of 24 squares. Make the number of squares needed for the design. Fasten off and sew in any yarn ends. The main sample design used the Block Square design (see page 37) but any motif can be used.

Top Tips

Turn this tote design into a cute vintage-style shopper by replacing the long straps with wooden handles. If you do use wooden handles, make sure to leave small side slits at the top when joining the bag. You will also need to replace step C in Joining the Bag Body with additional rows of double crochet on each panel edge to secure the wooden handles. You will need enough fabric to wrap through the handles and join together.

YARN WEIGHT:
Aran (worsted)

HOOK SIZE:
4mm/US size G-6
(or to match tension)

TENSION:
One single square motif =
10 x 10cm (4 x 4in)

SIZE:
Variable, to cover a canvas tote bag, which is used as the liner.

SAMPLE DESIGNS:
Two design variations, both worked in cotton aran-weight yarn:

Main make: Block Squares; long handles; worked in six colours.

Variation: Granny Squares; wooden handles; worked in a random colour mix using scraps.

APPROXIMATE METERAGE:
Total = 300m (328yd)

TOTAL SQUARES:
24 (for a standard tote bag, can vary).

TOTE BAG
Step by Step Pattern Guide

JOIN - MAKE TWO PANELS

PLACE ON TOTE TO WORK OUT EXTENSION ROWS NEEDED

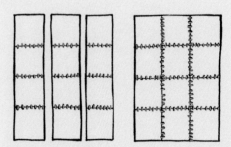

WORK EXTENSION ROWS

ADD FINAL EDGING ROUND

JOIN THE TWO PANELS TOGETHER AND ADD EDGE ROW TO THE OPENING

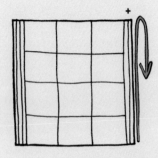
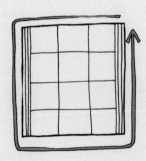
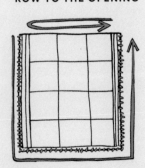

MAKE TWO STRAPS AND SPIKE STITCH EDGE

ATTACH STRAPS AND ADD TOTE LINER

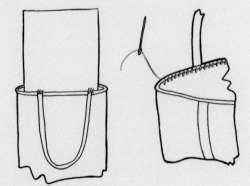

COLOURWAY

Five colours are used along with a black edging and border. Work each of the squares in a block colour. Divide the total number of squares by the number of colours used for an even spread of colours.

Instructions

MAKING UP
Use the joining and edging colour to make up your bag body.

BAG BODY PANELS
Main panels
A   Join your squares together into two panels using the double crochet joining technique (see page 63). First, join the short edges into rows and then join the longer rows together. Don't worry if they don't totally cover the tote at this stage.
B   Lay the rectangle of 12 squares on the tote to see how much of the area still needs to be covered.

Extension rows
Repeat this process for both panels.
A   For each 5cm (2in) gap in the width add an extension row to each side of your crochet panel. Follow the same stitch pattern as used the for the outer round of your squares. You can also add rows to the top and bottom of the panel if needed.
B   Repeat the extension rows as many times as necessary to cover the sides of the tote.

Edging
Double crochet around each side of the rectangular panels.
A   Start with the edging colour on your hook.
B   Join with a slip stitch into any corner stitch.
C   Chain 1.
D   Double crochet into each stitch along the edge (if you are working over the side of trebles, work 2 double crochets on the side of each treble post).
E   In corner stitches, (double crochet, chain, double crochet).
F   Repeat steps D and E until you reach the corner you started in.
G   Join into the first chain with a slip stitch to complete the round.
H   Fasten off.

JOINING THE BAG BODY
A   Place both panels right sides together and, using the same colour as for the edging, join the three edges together using the double crochet joining technique, leave the top open.
B   Turn the pouch right side out and join into a stitch along the open edge with a slip stitch.
C   Chain 1.
D   Double crochet into each stitch along the top edge to add a final round.
E   Join into the first stitch with a slip stitch to complete the round.
F   Fasten off and sew in yarn ends.

HANDLES
Repeat the pattern for each strap. Use two of the colours used in your squares.
A   Chain 90 + 1 turning chain. This is the length of your bag handle.
B   Miss 1 stitch, double crochet into each stitch along the row, turn the work.
C   Continue working in rows, chain 1, double crochet back along the row up to the end.
D   Repeat step C three more times and then fasten off.
E   Using the joining and edging colour, add a spike stitch edging around all sides of the handle to add strength.
F   Join in at the edge, starting 3 stitches and 3 rows in and work spike stitch following the instructions on page 68.
G   In corners work, (3 spike stitches, 1 chain, 3 spike stitches) into the same place to turn.
H   Stitches should line up with each other along both sides.
I   Fasten off.
J   Repeat steps A to I to make a second handle.
K   Attach the handles to the body of the bag using a double crochet join along the inside edge.

LINING
A   Cut the handles off the original canvas tote bag.
B   Place the canvas tote bag inside the crochet pouch and use whip stitch (see page 62) in the same colour as the edging to sew around the top edge of the bag to secure the lining in place.
C   Fasten off and sew in yarn ends.

ROLL NECK DICKIE BIB

The Roll Neck Dickie Bib is a sweater-scarf hybrid. It's the perfect piece to wear under a favourite jacket that you can't quite squeeze your sweater sleeves into, or it's a great option if you get fed up with constantly re-wrapping your scarf around your neck. A layering wardrobe staple!

YARN WEIGHT:
Aran (worsted)

HOOK SIZE:
4.5mm/US size 7
(or to match tension)

TENSION:
Four round square motif =
12 x 12cm (4¾ x 4¾in)

SIZE:
One size. Flat body =
52cm (20½in) across

SAMPLE DESIGN:
Aran wool yarn, Block Squares
in 10 colours worked in
alternating colour pairs.

APPROXIMATE METERAGE:
Total = 1000m (1094yd)

TOTAL SQUARES:
Ten extended squares (2 sizes).

Top Tips

Switch square designs and make the bib in the extended Granny Square (see page 33) for a different look.

Use up your odds and ends from this make by add fringing to the bottom edge or neck edge.

ROLL NECK DICKIE BIB
Step by Step Pattern Guide

BIB JOIN

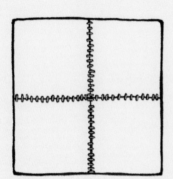

NECK JOIN

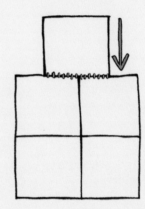

SHOULDER JOIN

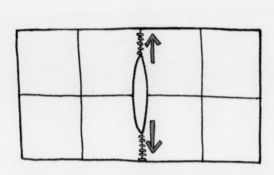

FINISHING

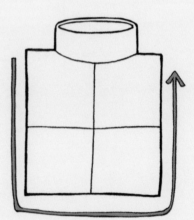

Getting Started

SQUARES

Make eight 10-round extended squares (bib body).
Make two 11-round extended squares (roll neck).
The sample is in the Block Square design (see page 37) but could also be made in the Granny Square pattern (see page 33).

COLOURWAY

Squares are made in contrasting colour pairs.
Make two squares in each colour combination but change the starting round colour in the second square to switch the colour balance. This produces a pair of squares that use the same colours but finish in the opposite colour to one another.

Instructions

JOINS

Join the squares in black yarn to give
a contrasting stitch effect.

Bib front and back join

A   Use the double crochet joining technique (see page 63) to join four (one of each colourway) of the 10-round squares together to make the bib front.
B   Repeat using the remaining four 10-round squares to complete the bib back.

Neck join

A   Add one 11-round square (which will become the roll neck) onto the centre top of each joined bib panel.
B   Line up the centre of the square with the bib centre join and double crochet join along the edge.
C   Repeat for other side of the bib.
D   Placing wrong sides of both panels together, use a double crochet join to stitch the sides of the roll neck together on the right side of the garment – remember to leave the head hole open.

Shoulder join

A   Turn the piece inside out.
B   On the wrong side of the bib use a double crochet join to stitch the remaining two open shoulder seams together.

Finishing

A   Join in with a with a slip stitch, chain 1 at the shoulder chain space.
B   Double crochet into each stitch and chain space of the bib body, work, (1 double crochet, 1 chain, 1 double crochet) into the bib corners.
C   Repeat until you are back at the starting stitch.
D   Join with a slip stitch into the first chain.
E   Fasten off.
F   Sew in yarn ends.

FINGERLESS MITTENS

The perfect glove that leaves your fingers free, handy for any outdoor cool-day crocheting! Fingerless mittens are a quick make perfect for using up your odds and ends of yarn. This project uses only four squares, so it is also super speedy. Why not make them in the same colourway as the scarf on page 143 to make a winter set?

YARN WEIGHT:
Aran (worsted)

HOOK SIZE:
4.5mm/US size 7
(or to match tension)

TENSION:
One single square motif =
12 x 12cm (4¾ x 4¾in).

SIZE:
One size: 12cm (4¾in) wide
by 18cm (7in) long.

SAMPLE DESIGN:
Aran wool yarn, Spot Squares
in eight colours, worked in a
random mix.

APPROXIMATE METERAGE:
Total = 120m (132 yd)

TOTAL SQUARES:
Four.

Top Tip

Ensure that you double crochet loosely around the thumb hole and mitten edge. Try the mittens on regularly during the making process to be sure they fit.

Lengthen the cuffs by creating a longer rib foundation chain.

FINGERLESS MITTENS
Step by Step Pattern Guide

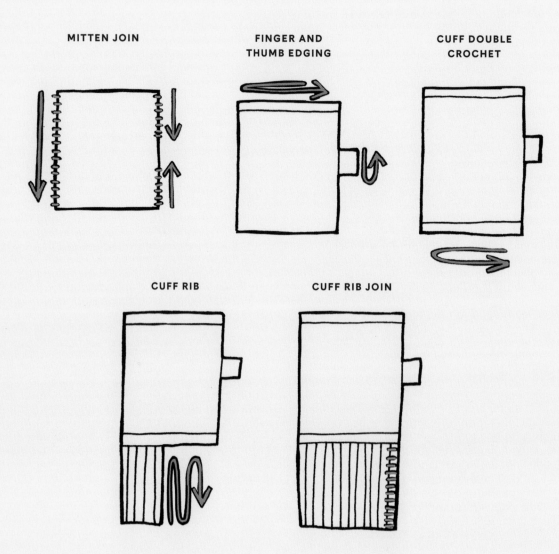

MITTEN JOIN

FINGER AND
THUMB EDGING

CUFF DOUBLE
CROCHET

CUFF RIB

CUFF RIB JOIN

Getting Started

SQUARES
Make four squares in the square design of your choice, the sample is made in the Spot Square (see page 41).

COLOURWAY
Change colour for each round of the motif and each part of the mitten, mix the colours evenly.

Instructions

Repeat the instructions for each fingerless mitten.

Mitten
A   Take two motif squares.
B   Working on the wrong side and starting in a corner chain space, double crochet two squares together (see page 63) down one side, stitching along the edge up to the next corner (14 double crochets in total).
C   Join in on the opposite edge and double crochet join 6 stitches up the side from the bottom, fasten off.
D   Join in at the top of the same side and double crochet join 4 stitches down from the top, fasten off.
E   The break in the joined edge creates a thumb space.

Finger edging
A   On the right side of the work, join in a new colour in any corner chain space along the top edge.
B   Chain 1, double crochet into each stitch and chain space along the round.
C   Join with a slip stitch into the first stitch to complete the round.
D   Repeat steps B–C once more.
E   Fasten off.

Thumb edging
A   Join in a new colour at a join stitch on the right side of the work.
B   Chain 1, double crochet into each stitch and join stitch along the round, working to create a round over both squares.
C   Join with a slip stitch into the first stitch to complete the round.
D   Repeat steps B–C twice more.
E   Fasten off.

Cuffs
A   On right side of the work, join in a new colour along the bottom edge in any corner chain space.
B   Chain 1, double crochet into each stitch and chain space along the round.
C   Join with a slip stitch into the first stitch to complete the round.
D   Chain 10 to create the foundation for a 9-stitch rib cuff.
E   Miss 1 chain, double crochet into the remaining 9 stitches of the chain.
F   Double crochet anchor into the next 2 stitches on mitten.
G   Turn the work, miss 2 stitches.
H   Working through the back of the loop, double crochet 9 stitches.
I   Continue following the rib technique, see page 69.
J   When the round is complete, double crochet join (see page 63) the first and the last row together on the wrong side of the work.
K   Fasten off.

Finishing
Sew in yarn ends.

TABLE SET

Brighten up your dining table with this quick make and give your 'table scaping' that crochet touch! This handmade table mat and coaster set provides the perfect backdrop for any meal, and works up brilliantly in raffia, cotton or tape yarn.

YARN WEIGHT:
Aran (worsted)

HOOK SIZE:
4.5mm/US size 7
(or to match tension)

TENSION:
One single square motif =
11 x 11cm (4¼ x 4¼in)

SIZE:
Coaster: 12.5 x 12.5cm (5 x 5in)
Mat: 28 x 39cm (11 x 15¼in)

SAMPLE DESIGN:
Raffia yarn, Spot Squares
in four colours, worked in
a random mix.

APPROXIMATE METERAGE:
Total (set of four) =
800m (875yd)

Per coaster/mat set =
200m (219yd)

TOTAL SQUARES:
One set = seven squares.
One coaster = one square.
One mat = six squares.

Top Tip

You could work in a cotton aran yarn instead to create a washable set!

Make a matching table runner by increasing the number of squares in your rows before edging.

TABLE SET
Step by Step Pattern Guide

COASTER EDGING

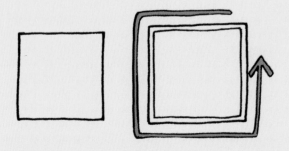

MAT JOIN

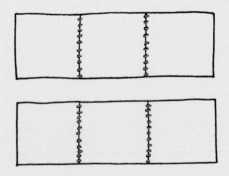

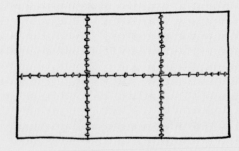

MAT BORDER EDGING

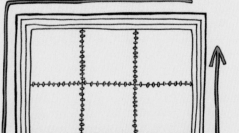

PICOT FINAL EDGE

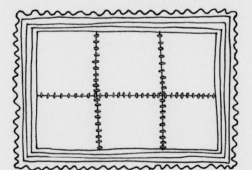

Getting Started

SQUARES

Make seven squares per coaster and mat set, for a set of four you will need 28 squares. Fasten off and sew in yarn ends. The sample design uses the Spot Square (page 41), but any square can be used. If you are using raffia the squares can be very misshapen before blocking, block after edging.

COLOURWAY

Use four colours and change colour each round. Work each square in a different colour order and try to mix colours evenly across the set.

Instructions

COASTER

Edge each single square with a double crochet edge (see page 67).

A   Join in with a slip stitch at any corner point.
B   Chain 2, double crochet into the same corner point.
C   Double crochet into each stitch along the edge.
D   (Double crochet, chain, double crochet) into the corner.
E   Repeat steps C and D until you reach the first chain.
F   Join with a slip stitch into the first chain. Fasten off.
G   Sew in yarn tail to complete.

MAT

Join six squares together in two rows of three using the double crochet joining technique (see page 63).

A   First join the squares together at the short edges, to create two strips of three.
B   Join the strips together along the long central edge to create a mat.

Edging

Work three rounds of double crochet edge around the mat, changing colour for each round.

A   Join in with a slip stitch at any corner chain space.
B   Work 1 double crochet into each stitch along the edge.
C   (Double crochet, chain, double crochet) into corner chain space.
D   Repeat steps B and C until you reach the first chain of the round.
E   Join with a slip stitch into the first chain. Fasten off.
F   Repeat steps A to E twice more, changing colour for each round.
G   Edge the final round in a new colour working the picot edge (see page 66).
H   Join with a slip stitch into the first chain. Fasten off.
I   Sew in any remaining ends.

BLOCK

Block your crochet (see page 74) to finish the set off. If you are working in raffia your work may be misshapen and may not lie flat. Due to the type of yarn used, you can block this project slightly differently to other pieces. With most natural raffia yarns, you can press iron them in the blocking process, using a small amount of steam to create crisp, flat mats. If you do intend to use this technique, please test it out on a small sample first to make sure you won't damage your final piece! You can also place a tea towel over the piece during the blocking process to protect it.

SUPPLIERS   THANKS

Support your local yarn stores where you can! Here's a run down of the yarns I used for my project samples:

Simple Square Sweater – Feeling Good Yarn, Wool and the Gang and Paintbox Yarns 100% Worsted Wool, Lovecrafts.com/Paintbox Yarns Cotton Aran, Lovecrafts.com

Pick N Mix sweater – Paintbox Yarns Simply DK, Lovecrafts.com/StyleCraft Special DK

Bucket hat – Feeling Good Yarn, Wool and the Gang/ Paintbox Yarns Cotton Aran, Lovecrafts.com

Quilt Cardy – Alpachino Merino, Wool and the Gang/ Hayfield Bonus DK (2 strands), Sirdar

Lazy daisy top – Paintbox Yarns Cotton DK, Lovecrafts.com

Spot and stripes blanket – Paintbox Yarns Simply Chunky, Lovecrafts.com

Collar – Paintbox Yarns DK Cotton/Paintbox Yarns 100% Wool Worsted, Lovecrafts.com

Pouch bag – Ra-Ra Rafia, Wool and the Gang

Graphic grid cushion – Paintbox Yarns Simply Chunky, Lovecrafts.com

Groovy Granny cardy – StyleCraft Special DK/ Paintbox Yarns Simply DK, Lovecrafts.com

Tie-back top – Paintbox Yarns DK Cotton, Lovecrafts.com

Sweater vest – Paintbox Yarns Aran Cotton/Paintbox Yarns 100% Wool Worsted, Lovecrafts.com

Scarf – Paintbox Yarns Wool Mix Super Chunky, Lovecrafts.com

Beret – StyleCraft Special DK

Square skirt and top – Must Have 4 Ply, Yarn and Colors/ Rainbow Cotton 8/4 Color Pack, Hobbii.co.uk

Graphic grid blanket – Paintbox Yarns Simply Chunky, Lovecrafts.com

Tote bag – Paintbox Yarns Cotton Aran, Lovecrafts.com

Roll neck dickie bib – Paintbox Yarns 100% Wool Worsted, Lovecrafts.com

Fingerless mittens – Paintbox Yarns 100% Wool Worsted, Lovecrafts.com

Table set – Ra-Ra Rafia, Wool and the Gang

My first thank you is to you, yes you! Thank you for reading this book! You're the best and I hope this helps you make some amazing crochet that you love and cherish!

To anyone that has ever come to a workshop, bought a pattern or just left an Insta Like, thank you for helping me get to this point – it really is a dream come true!

A massive thank you to my amazing models who rocked that crochet so well! You were all fantastic – Euan Roberts, Amanda Lyddon (aka Grannie Duck), Sara Brown, Mara Livermore, Deborah and Grace Latter, Lily Kim, Nona Ahamat, Elisha Edwards, my two fave Toms and Nell Gransden for stepping in, too!

To the amazing team that put this book together, Kajal and all those at Hardie Grant that made this dream happen. Thank you for understanding my Granny Square obsession and for all your support during this project.

To my bestie and wonderful photographer, Rachel Manns – thank you for being my absolute rock during this project. To my editor, Chelsea, and art director, Claire, working with you both, alongside Rachel, was the best dream team I could ask for! Thank you so much for all your help through this project that ran through a rollercoaster time for me. You have all been beyond amazing and supportive, thank you!

The hugest thanks to my mumma, Annie, for all the hundreds of hours crocheting with me, your modelling skills and all round amazingness, I couldn't do any of this without you! To my husband, Tom, for the constant support, cups of tea, dinners and even begrudged modelling, love you lots! And a general big thank you to all my family and friends who I have ignored while I was busy crocheting away!

Thanks to Wool and the Gang for providing some yarn support!

And lastly a big thank you to my hands, for all the crochet hours they put in this year – it was a massive job and you did not fail me, I promise rest and a manicure as a treat!

This book is dedicated to my Grandad Bill who I miss massively and who was my biggest cheerleader.

xxxx